THE WIZARD
OF CAUSE

A path to remembering your wholeness

Dr. Heidi Heron PsyD

© 2025 Heidi Heron

All rights reserved.

No part of this publication may be reproduced, distributed, or transmitted in any form or by any means, including photocopying, recording, or other electronic or mechanical methods, without the prior written permission of the author, except in the case of brief quotations embodied in critical reviews and certain other non-commercial uses permitted by copyright law.

First Edition

Published by NLP Worldwide
Sydney, Australia
www.nlpworldwide.com
www.wizardofcause.com
www.heidiheron.com

ISBN: 978-1-7643581-0-1

This is a work of fiction. Names, characters, places, and incidents either are products of the author's imagination or are used fictitiously. Any resemblance to actual persons, living or dead, or actual events is purely coincidental.

For more reflections, journal prompts, and resources inspired by this book, visit www.wizardofcause.com

Table of Contents

Chapter 1 The Fog of Should 1

Chapter 2: The Compass 4

Chapter 3 The Keeper of the Room 8

Chapter 4 The First Map 16

Chapter 5 The Market of Masks 27

Chapter 6 The Garden of Echoes 35

Chapter 7 The Temple of Time 46

Chapter 8 The Tower of Titles 57

Chapter 9 The House of Mirrors 65

Chapter 10 The Return 73

Chapter 11 The Quiet Yes 82

Chapter 12 The Map Rewritten 90

Chapter 13 The Cost of Clarity 98

Chapter 14 The North Star 107

Chapter 15 When the Old Self Calls 116

Chapter 16 The Invitation 125

Chapter 17 The Wizard of Cause 132

Chapter 18 The Map Continues 141

Reflections and Prompts 148

The Author – Dr. Heidi Heron PsyD 173

DEDICATION

To my clients, students, and friends -
we've walked this path together.
I've known what it is to live in Effect, chasing the illusion of getting it right.
And through you, I've remembered that freedom begins
not in fixing life, but in choosing it.
As I've helped you find your way,
you've helped me find mine.
Your courage to shift, to wake, to live from Cause -
it moves me, teaches me, and continues to inspire my own becoming.

PREFACE

A Path to Remembering Your Wholeness

We are taught to chase control.
To fix, to prove, to please, to perform.
To make ourselves small enough to be liked and strong enough to be needed.

We learn to measure our worth in productivity, approval, and perfection.
We call this life. We call this success.
But for many of us… it never quite fits.

This is a book about what happens when we stop performing and start listening.
To the quiet ache.
To the lost map.
To the compass inside us that still remembers what matters.

It's the story of Avery, a woman who begins to ask better questions.
Not because she's broken.
But because she's ready to stop disappearing inside a life that doesn't feel like her own.

As you follow her path, you may find pieces of yourself.
In the fog. In the masks. In the mirrors. In the maps.

You may begin to remember:
That wholeness was never something to earn.
It was always something to return to.

You may notice how often you've been living from Effect: reacting, complying, silencing your truth to keep the peace.
And you may begin, like Avery, to return to Cause.
To choose with awareness.

To live from what matters.
To trust yourself again.

Because wholeness isn't perfection.
It isn't performance.
It isn't being liked by everyone.

It's being lived-in by you.

This is the journey of remembering.
Of realigning.
Of becoming a Wizard of Cause.

And it begins right here.

— The Wizard of Cause —

CHAPTER 1
THE FOG OF SHOULD

Avery hadn't cried in over a year. Not because life had been kind, it hadn't, but because there simply hadn't been time. Each day unfolded like a checklist: wake before the alarm, get Milo ready for school, unload the dishwasher, pack the lunch, reply to emails, reheat the coffee, stir dinner, scroll headlines, set the alarm, sleep, and repeat.

She wasn't overwhelmed exactly. She was full. Full of decision fatigue. Full of noise. Full of the invisible weight of keeping everything running without letting anything fall apart. Her mind buzzed constantly, even in rest. Even in silence.

In the quiet moments, the ones between tasks when the hum of movement faded, there was a sound she didn't like. A low ache. Not a pain exactly, but a question that never formed into words. It was like a song she used to know but hadn't heard in so long, she wasn't sure it had ever existed. And yet it tugged at her, familiar and faint.

Outside, the world applauded her. "You're amazing. I don't know how you do it all." "You're so strong, Avery." "You're handling everything so well." She nodded, smiled, and said thank you. Then she logged into Zoom, smiled at her reflection, and answered emails about optimising workflows while her soul whispered, *What are we even doing here?* Her face on screen looked capable, composed. Her eyes didn't agree.

The work was fine. The people were fine. The pay was fine. She wasn't.

Milo was eight, sweet and observant. He'd started asking questions lately that made her stomach flip. "Why don't you laugh much anymore?" "Why are you tired?" "Do you enjoy your job?," His words were never accusatory, simply curious. Honest. She always found an answer. But she wasn't sure she ever found the truth.

The separation had been clean. That's what the lawyers called it. No courtroom, no fighting. Two lonely signatures and some labelled boxes. But clean wasn't the same as clear. What lingered was quieter. Less visible. The kind of heaviness you carry in your bones, not your hands.

Now there were two houses. Two toothbrushes. Two lives. Every week brought multiple transfers during the weekdays and every other weekend. The handovers were civil, respectful, yet exhausting. Each time she felt like she was dropping off half of her heart at someone else's door. Two days here, two days there, then three days back again – flipping each week like a never-ending dance. As soon as they'd settled, it was time to move again.

She didn't miss her ex, not in the way people expected. But she missed the distraction. She missed the second adult. She missed the illusion of a shared load. Most of all, she missed someone to blame, someone else to carry part of the weight. Now it was all on her, every decision, every deadline, every forgotten lunchbox and tearful bedtime.

And on nights like this, alone with her laptop open and an inbox full of unread requests she didn't care about, the fog crept in again.

It always started the same way. Avery would glance at the clock: 11:42 p.m. She'd wonder how it got so late. She'd think, *Just one more thing.* But instead of clicking, she'd sit still. Her hand would hover over the mouse. Then drop.

In the silence, the question would rise. *Is this it?* Not in a dramatic way. Not with violins or shouting, or even sadness, only a quiet, unshakable curiosity. *Is this the life I chose, or the one that happened to me?*

She pushed the thought away with dishes or deadlines or double-choc ice-cream, but it always came back. It rolled in like fog through the cracks in the windows, quiet, cold, and impossible to hold. Some nights, she barely noticed it. Other nights, like this one, it sat with her.

That night, something unusual happened. As Avery shut her laptop and stood to turn off the light, she noticed a small, folded paper on the floor near the couch. It wasn't hers. At least, she didn't remember dropping it. The light caught on the soft grey edge. She bent to pick it up.

It was blank on the outside, merely soft grey paper folded in half. Inside, in narrow handwriting, it said:

You are not lost. You are living by someone else's map.

There was no name. No explanation. Only those words.

Avery read it again. And again. The paper warmed slightly in her palm.

Then, for the first time in what felt like forever, she didn't go back to the to-do list. She sat down, held the note in both hands, and let the silence stretch. Not the urgent kind. The spacious kind. The kind that lets things rise.

Outside, the city slept. Inside, something stirred. The fog hadn't lifted. But something had shifted.

And somewhere deep inside her chest, something small and quiet asked, *What if there's another way?*

– A path to remembering your wholeness –

Chapter 2
The Compass

Avery kept the note. She told herself it was nothing – a leftover from Milo's school project, a misprint, a mistake. But the paper felt heavy in her hands, heavier than its size allowed, as if it carried a truth she hadn't been ready to hold. She tucked it into the drawer beside her bed, next to an old lip balm and a tangle of charger cables. It felt safer there, out of sight but not entirely out of reach. And then she did what she always did, she got on with it.

Emails. Traffic. Milo's lunch left on the counter. A message from his teacher about a misplaced book. The current of life swept her up again, fast and familiar. But something inside her felt out of sync. It was subtle, like a skipped beat in a favourite song. She felt half a second behind everything, as if her sound and picture were out of alignment, or as though she was moving through her life with the volume turned down.

That afternoon, Milo had been picked up by his dad. Overnight bag packed, water bottle full, Frank, his favourite stuffed dinosaur poking out the top. He hugged Avery tight at the door, his cheek warm against her neck. "Love you, Mom." "Love you too, kiddo." He didn't cry. He rarely did. But he looked back twice as he walked toward the car, and that was enough to leave her chest aching. The flat always felt quieter when he was gone. Not simply silent, still. As if the air itself missed him.

By Thursday evening, the fog had thickened again. After the dishes were done and the sun had gone down, Avery poured a cup of tea she didn't want, and stood at the window, staring at the apartment buildings across the street. Most windows were dark. A few flickered with television glow. All of them looked like scenes from lives she wasn't part of. She pressed her forehead to the glass. It was cool against her skin. Her reflection looked tired. Not broken, faded. As though she was going through the motions in a story she didn't remember agreeing to. She sighed and turned away.

That's when she saw it: a small, round, metallic shape on the kitchen bench. It hadn't been there before. It wasn't hers, and it wasn't Milo's. Her feet moved before her mind caught up. She picked it up and turned it over in her palm. It was a compass. Old, scratched, and cold in her hand. But somehow, it felt alive. There was a quiet hum in her fingertips, as if the object was aware of her. She turned it over. No markings. No brand. Only one simple engraving:

Not North.

Avery let out a short, startled laugh. What kind of compass didn't point north?

The needle spun lazily, like it was waking from a long nap. Then it stopped. Not at N, E, S, or W, but slightly off to the side. Just left of centre. Toward the bookshelf. She blinked. Her body remained still, but something in her chest leaned forward. She stepped closer. The needle twitched.

She stood in front of the bookshelf. Her eyes scanned the rows: parenting books, leadership guides, half-read novels, and a stack of journals she meant to fill but never did. The compass pointed upward. She reached for the top shelf and pulled down a thin, fabric-covered journal. It was blank. She didn't remember buying it. Didn't remember placing it there. But there it was, soft in her hands, the fabric worn smooth at the corners as if it had been waiting for her.

She flipped through the pages. Empty. Clean. The paper was thick and quiet beneath her touch. Then one slip of grey parchment fluttered out and landed at her feet. It was the same narrow handwriting as before:

The compass doesn't find the way. It listens to what matters.

Avery sat down on the floor, tea forgotten. The tiles were cool beneath her legs. She opened the journal to the first page, grabbed her favourite pen from the drawer beside the fridge, and wrote, almost without thinking, *What matters to me?* She stared at the question. It looked like someone else had written it. Someone braver.

She tried to answer. She wrote: *Milo.* Then nothing. Her mind filled with static. Obligations. Opinions. Old advice. Her mother's voice. Her boss's. Her ex's. Her own voice, reminding her to be grateful, reminding her this was enough. But the page stayed mostly blank.

She closed the journal, her hand trembling slightly, and held the compass again. The needle spun. Then it stopped. This time it pointed toward the front door. She frowned, her body tensing slightly. Before she could move, three soft knocks echoed through the apartment. Not loud. Purely certain.

She froze. It was past midnight. She wasn't expecting anyone. She wasn't dressed for company. She wasn't even sure she was fully awake. Three more taps.

She grabbed the closest thing, a soft cardigan from the back of a chair, and wrapped it around herself. Her fingers hesitated on the latch. Then she opened the door a crack. No one. Only silence. And on the doormat, a small envelope. Same handwriting.

Inside: *Maps are made by those who walk without one.*

— *The Wizard of Cause* —

Avery stepped outside. The air was still, unusually warm for autumn. There was a strange hush in the night, as though the city itself was holding its breath. Down the street, beneath a flickering streetlight, a figure stood. Still.
Not threatening. Waiting.

Before she could call out, the figure turned and walked away. Avery looked down at the compass. The needle pointed after them. She didn't know why, but she followed. Shoes on. Keys in hand. No plan.
Simply something whispering, *Go.*

– A path to remembering your wholeness –

Chapter 3
The Keeper of the Room

She followed the compass through quiet streets and sleeping city blocks, her breath steady, her pace unsure. The night wrapped around her like a question she didn't yet know how to answer. She didn't know what she was walking toward — only that she couldn't stay still anymore.

Eventually, the compass stilled. The needle pointed toward a narrow alley, one she didn't remember noticing before. She hesitated at the entrance, glancing up at the old streetlamp flickering above her, then stepped in.

Halfway down, nestled between stone and shadow, was a door. Not grand. Not glowing. Just... there. Plain wood. Worn edges. No sign. No handle. But it pulled at her somehow – as if it had always been waiting, and she had only become the version of herself who could see it.

It seemed out of place, and yet entirely meant to be there. After a final glance behind her, she stepped forward and pressed her hand to the wood.

The door didn't creak. It sighed: a soft exhale of time and invitation, as if it had been waiting a long time to be opened.

She stepped inside slowly, bracing herself for dust, cobwebs, forgotten things. Instead, she found stillness. The room was warm. The walls were stone, worn smooth by age or care. A soft light glowed from nowhere in particular, illuminating a wooden table in the centre. On it sat a steaming pot of tea and two cups. No one else was in sight.

She frowned, unsettled by the quiet arrangement. "What is this?" she asked aloud. Her voice echoed slightly, sounding louder than she expected. No answer came, only the gentle pop of the teapot, as if it had now finished brewing.

Avery took a cautious step forward, then paused. The room was too tidy. Too prepared. Too intentional. It felt set up, and her gut braced for something hidden. She wasn't used to being invited into things she didn't have to manage, fix, or prove herself worthy of. Her eyes scanned the walls, half expecting a warning, or a condition scrawled in neat script.

Then a voice, calm and dry, drifted from the corner. It was somehow familiar, like a melody she couldn't place. "Welcome."

A woman stepped forward from the shadows. Her grey hair hung in a loose braid. Her hands looked as though they had worked with earth or thread, maybe both. Her eyes were steady, deep-set, as if they had seen through time and decided not to interrupt it. She wore layered, soft clothing, the kind chosen for comfort, worn unapologetically, not for show.

Avery instinctively straightened her cardigan. "Hi," she said. "Um… what is this place?"

The woman smiled with the ease of someone who didn't rush to explain. "Some call it a room. Some call it a threshold. I call it useful."

Avery blinked. "That's not an answer."

"No," the woman replied. "It's an invitation."

Avery crossed her arms, more out of habit than intention. "An invitation? I'm not here for anything… weird."

The woman raised an eyebrow gently. "And yet, you walked through a hidden door carrying a compass that pointed you to it."

Avery didn't respond. The logic was too inconvenient.

The woman gestured toward the chair. "Sit. Or don't. But the tea's at its best now."

Something in Avery bristled at the offer. Hospitality without expectation felt foreign. She didn't trust things that arrived without effort. Her life had been built on earning everything: rest, love, space, stability. Even compliments made her skin twitch. She hovered near the chair but didn't sit.

Her voice came out sharper than she intended. "I'm guessing you're some kind of guide."

The woman tilted her head thoughtfully. "You don't trust guides?"

"I don't trust people who say they can help," Avery said. "Most of the time, it simply means they want to fix you. Or save you. Or sell you something."

The woman didn't flinch. "I don't fix. I don't save. I don't sell."

"Then what do you do?" Avery asked.

"I remind," the woman said.

Avery hesitated, then sat. The chair was softer than she expected, almost welcoming. She didn't touch the tea. The woman didn't push. She simply waited, letting the silence breathe.

Then, almost casually, she said, "You've been living in Effect."

Avery blinked. "Is that some woo-woo way of saying I'm stuck?"

"No," the woman replied calmly. "It's a very clear way of saying you've been reacting to life, instead of responding from yourself."

Avery frowned, not quite sure whether she felt challenged or seen. "What's the difference?"

The woman reached for the teapot and poured herself a cup with quiet care. Her movements were unhurried, present. "Effect is when your sense of worth, peace, or power depends on what's happening around you – who shows up, what goes wrong, what someone thinks of you. Cause is when you choose who you want to be, even when the world doesn't play along."

Avery looked away, then back. "You make it sound easy."

"Not easy," the woman said, her voice even. "Available."

There was a long pause. The tea between them gently steamed. The room seemed to hold its own kind of breath.

After a sip from her cup, the woman gazed at Avery. "To begin to live at Cause, you need to know what matters most to you. What you want."

Avery's voice dropped to a whisper. "What if I don't know?"

The woman smiled gently, no trace of judgment. "Then we start there." She leaned forward, not forceful, but real. "You don't have to figure it all out today. But you do need to stop outsourcing your identity to everything that hurts you."

Avery looked down at her hands. She didn't know what to say. The words weren't a revelation. They were a recognition. She had been living like a weathervane, spinning in the direction of every deadline, every demand, every disapproving glance. It was exhausting. And she hadn't even realised how much of it she had mistaken for strength.

The woman reached into her pocket and placed something on the table, a small, folded square of parchment. "For later," she said. "When the noise quiets."

Avery didn't open it right away. She simply nodded, unsure why her chest felt both warm and hollow at the same time.

That night, Avery didn't sleep much. She lay in bed replaying the conversation in her mind. She didn't journal. Didn't plan. Didn't try to solve. But before sunrise, she found herself whispering into the dark, **"Then we start there."**

When Avery opened the journal the next morning to a fresh blank page, words began to appear softly, steadily, as if the page already knew what needed to be said. The handwriting was the same as the earlier notes. But this time, it wasn't just a sentence. It was a message.

— *The Wizard of Cause* —

The moment before change rarely feels like magic.

It usually feels like something's off, but you can't name what.
You might feel stuck. Or tired. Or like you're performing a life that used to fit, but now... doesn't.

Most people think transformation begins with a lightning bolt. A big decision. A dramatic shift.
But often, it starts in silence. In discomfort.
In a flicker of awareness that says, "This isn't it anymore."

Even if nothing looks different on the outside, something inside you is already shifting.
You're noticing patterns.
You're questioning roles.
You're wondering who you are when you're not performing, fixing, pleasing, or proving.

– A path to remembering your wholeness –

That wondering?
It's sacred.

You don't need a dramatic plan.
You don't need to know exactly where you're going.
You only need one true step, a shift from autopilot to awareness.

That's when something else becomes possible:
Living from Cause.

It doesn't mean controlling everything.
It means choosing who you are, not what's expected of you.
It means recognising that while you can't always change your circumstances, you can choose how you meet them.

You can ask:

- Am I choosing this – or complying with it?
- Do I feel aligned – or obligated?
- What am I waiting for… that I could give myself?

Sometimes, the first act of Cause isn't action.
It's noticing.
It's pausing long enough to hear what your life is trying to tell you.

If you're not sure what to do next, start here:

Notice what no longer feels like you.

Pay attention to what brings relief, not approval.

Ask what might happen if you didn't rush to make everything okay.

— *The Wizard of Cause* —

This is how it begins.
Not loud.
But intentional.

You're not broken for feeling lost.
You're evolving.
And you're not behind.
You're exactly where your awareness is asking you to be.

– A path to remembering your wholeness –

Chapter 4
The First Map

Avery barely slept. She tried. She pulled the covers up to her chin, stared at the ceiling, even opened a meditation app she hadn't used since her last New Year's resolution. But the woman's words lingered.

"To live at Cause, you need to know what's important to you."

And that folded square of parchment, still unopened on her nightstand, seemed to pulse with a quiet insistence, as if it were holding something sacred. Or dangerous. Or both.

Right before dawn, she finally opened it.

The handwriting was the same as the other notes: looping, deliberate, and oddly familiar.

What matters the most to you?

Not what *should* matter. Not what her boss or her ex or her parents would approve of. What mattered to her.

And the truth?

She didn't know.

In the early hours, before Milo came home, before the inbox buzzed, Avery sat at the kitchen table in her dressing gown, tea in one hand and pen in the other. The compass sat silently beside her, as if it too were waiting. She opened the journal to a fresh page and wrote at the top: **What matters to me?**

Then she stared at it.

She didn't try to get it right. She simply started writing.

- **Milo** – that one came easy.
  Then…
- **Kindness**
- **Peace**
- **Time that doesn't feel rushed**
- **Being able to breathe without guilt**
- **Laughter that isn't forced**
- **Honesty, even when it's hard**

The words came in fragments. She didn't know if they were values, wishes, or crumbs from a life she used to recognise. But something about seeing them on the page made her feel less adrift.

She flipped to a new page and tried a different heading: **In my work, what matters?**

The old answers rose up first – achievement, recognition, security – but none of them felt true now. Not in her bones. So she wrote:

- Making something that matters
- Feeling like I'm not pretending
- Freedom over fame
- Purpose, not performance

Another heading: **In love…**

She hadn't been there in a while. But something inside her stirred.

- Safety
- Play
- Deep conversation
- Space
- Trust
- Knowing I can be me

That last one stopped her: **Knowing I can be me.**

And suddenly, she wasn't in her kitchen anymore.

She was eight.

Sitting cross-legged under the giant willow tree at her grandparents' farm, notebook in hand, drawing pictures of clouds with faces.

The air smelled like cut grass and river water.
The wind tugged at her hair.
She hummed like the world belonged to her.

Her grandmother leaned out from the back door.
"Still dreaming, little wizard?"

Avery grinned. "I'm making spells."

"What kind?"

"Spells that let people tell the truth and still be loved."

The memory hit like a warm ache.
She hadn't thought about that day in decades.
But now, it landed in her chest like a bell.

She turned to a fresh page and wrote, slowly:

I value space to be who I am – without having to shrink or explain.

The compass gave a soft click.

By the time the sky had begun to lighten and the tea had gone cold beside her, Avery had filled five pages.

She heard the quiet knock on the door, followed by the low hum of a car engine still running outside. When she opened it, Milo stood beside his dad, holding Frank, hair a little mussed from sleep and the seatbelt.

"Morning," his dad said, offering a polite smile. "He's had breakfast. Everything's in the bag."

Avery nodded, her eyes on Milo. "Thanks."

Milo stepped forward and wrapped his arms around her waist. She crouched and held him tightly, breathing in the scent of shampoo and something faintly citrus, his dad's aftershave, maybe. He felt heavier than yesterday, like he'd grown overnight. Or maybe it was that she hadn't realised how much she missed him.

"Welcome home," she whispered.

He smiled against her shoulder, then pulled back. "What's all the paper for?" he asked, pointing past her to the table where the journal and compass waited.

"Just writing," she said, brushing a hand through his hair.

"Is it for work?"

"No," she replied, smiling softly. "It's for me."

He stepped inside, dropped his backpack, and wandered toward the kitchen.

"Cool," he said, already reaching for his game console lying on the counter.

Avery watched him for a moment before closing the door. As she sat down at the table, something inside her settled. She could hold this, her own becoming, and her love for him, at the same time. Maybe it was okay to choose herself, and still show up for the ones she loved.

Later that afternoon, Avery sent a quick message to Maya.

Maya had known Milo since he was born. She was part friend, part honorary aunt, the kind of person who always had snacks in her bag and somehow knew how to talk to kids without talking down to them. She arrived with a puzzle book, a packet of popcorn, and her usual grin.

"You've got that look," Maya said as she stepped inside.

Avery raised an eyebrow. "What look?"

"The *something's stirring* look."

Avery smiled faintly. "Maybe it is."

Milo lit up when he saw her. "Maya!"

He wrapped his arms around her waist and immediately started telling her about dinosaurs, cereal rankings, and a dream involving a talking kangaroo.

"I won't be long," Avery said, grabbing her bag and slipping the compass into her coat pocket.

Maya waved her off. "Go. We're good."

And with that, Avery stepped out the door, heart racing for reasons she didn't quite understand. She didn't know exactly where she was going, only that something was calling her back.

Following her senses and the compass, she returned to the door she had found the night before. The lights inside the room were dimmer now. The air felt quieter somehow, as if the room had taken a long breath in her absence.

The woman was waiting.

"Well?" she asked, motioning to the journal in Avery's hands.

"I wrote what matters," Avery said, offering it forward.

The woman didn't open it. She placed it gently on the table instead.

"You made your first map."

"I don't know if they're the right answers," Avery said, crossing her arms again.

"They're not supposed to be right," the woman replied. "They're supposed to be yours."

Avery glanced around the room again. It was too tidy, too warm, too prepared. She hesitated, then sighed.

"Look," she said finally. "I've done therapy. Coaching. Journaling. I've read the books, okay?"

"I believe you," the woman said softly.

"I'm not here to be cracked open."

"No one's trying to break you," she replied. "But maybe something in you is ready to open."

Avery scoffed lightly. "You make it sound as though I'm about to bloom."

The woman didn't flinch. "Maybe you are. But first, something has to take root and grow."

She reached beneath the table and pulled out a piece of parchment. On it, handwritten in ink that shimmered faintly in the light, were five simple words:

What do you value most?

Avery stared at it as if it had accused her of something.

"What kind of question is that?"

"That depends," the woman said.

"On what?"

"On who's asking. On who's watching. On who might be disappointed by your answer." She leaned in slightly, her voice steady. "It depends on whether you're trying to impress… or align."

Avery exhaled sharply. "Great, more cryptic wisdom to unravel."

"It's not cryptic," the woman said. "It's a mirror."

Avery looked at her through narrowed eyes, measuring the words, testing for sincerity. Then she glanced down at the note again. "I don't even know what that word means anymore, *value*. It gets thrown around like some kind of brand strategy. A virtue checklist."

The woman nodded gently. "That's not unusual. Most people confuse values with ideals. Or rules. Or what they think they *should* care about." She continued. "Values aren't what look good on paper. They're what feel right in your bones. They're what ache when you abandon them. They're the things you protect – even when no one's watching."

Avery was quiet.

"They're not fixed," the woman added. "They can grow with you. But when you live against them for too long, you start to feel lost. Or resentful. Or numb. Not because you've failed, but because you've drifted too far from yourself."

The words weren't new. But they didn't feel like advice. They felt like remembering.

The woman moved to a wide cabinet and opened it. Inside were shelves stacked with journals, hand-bound, faded, and delicate. She pulled open one of the lower drawers, revealing rows of books lying flat, each resting in its own shallow tray.

Some were neat, with precise lines and careful lettering. Some were chaotic: scribbles, jagged ink, pages warped and worn. Some were filled with colour. Others held only a few scattered words.

"These are the maps of those who came before you."

Avery stepped closer. She felt something reverent in the room. Not sacred, but honest.

"Some people never finish their map," the woman said. "Some don't even start."

"And the ones who do?"

"They don't find their way – they create it."

She turned and placed a small stone in Avery's palm. It was warm, as if it had been sitting in the sun. "One value," she said. "One truth. One anchor."

Avery looked down. A single word appeared, slowly, carved into the surface: *Space*. She looked up, her voice soft. "How did it know?"

The woman smiled. "Because you finally made some."

That night, long after Milo had gone to bed, Avery opened her journal. She didn't fill a page. She didn't make a list. She wrote:
I want to matter to myself.

Then added:
Not for what I do. But for who I am.

She closed the journal and let that be enough. The compass, resting on the table beside her, ticked once. Then turned. Not wildly. Not erratically. A quiet shift. East, maybe. Or somewhere close.

It didn't matter.

Because for the first time in a long time, Avery did.

– A path to remembering your wholeness –

What Really Matters

Let's get clear.

A value is anything that's deeply important to you.

Not what looks good on a slide.
Not what earns approval.
Not what someone else says should matter.

Just what feels true, in your body, in your bones.

Values are the invisible architecture of your alignment.
They're the thread beneath your choices, your peace, and your unease.

You'll feel them most clearly when they're either fully honoured...
or painfully ignored.

When a value is met, something in you relaxes.
You feel grounded. Energised. At ease.

When a value is denied, even subtly, your body knows.
Tight shoulders. Shallow breath. A quiet ache that whispers, "This isn't it."

Because even if the box is ticked, your soul is not.

You can find values in every part of your life:

- **In love:** honesty, intimacy, freedom, support
- **In work:** autonomy, purpose, stability, creativity
- **In time:** spaciousness, flow, slowness, clarity
- **In health:** energy, mobility, strength, ease
- **In parenting:** presence, patience, guidance, fun

They don't have to be poetic or profound.
They only have to be true.

Here's where it gets interesting.

Most of us never stop to ask what our
values actually are.
We inherit them — from family,
schools, culture, systems.
We live by them without questioning.
We suffer by them without knowing why.

Until one day, we burn out.
Or feel numb.
Or snap at someone we love.
Or stare at the ceiling and think, this can't be it.

That's when the compass starts to twitch.

So, here's the invitation:

Pick three areas of your life right now – maybe work, love, and time. And ask yourself:

What's important to me about this area?

Are those values being met?

If not, what's one thing I could start, stop, or change to honour what matters?

Your answers don't need to be perfect.
They simply need to be yours.

Because once you name what really matters,
you stop outsourcing your peace.
You stop bending to what drains you.
You stop explaining yourself to people who wouldn't understand anyway.

Values aren't goals.

They're what make the goal worth it.

They're not branding.

They're belonging, to yourself.

And when things feel tangled again – because they will – you don't need to start over.

You return.

To what's important.
To what's true.
To your Cause.

Chapter 5
The Market of Masks

The next morning, after dropping Milo at his grandma's for the morning, Avery followed her usual walking path through the park. The compass in her pocket began to hum, not spinning, but pulsing, like a heartbeat. When she took it out, the needle didn't point north. It pointed ahead.

And there it was, the door she thought she'd dreamed. The one that didn't exist on any street map. She didn't question it.

Shoes on. Hair tied back. No makeup. No plan. Only a quiet knowing that this wasn't about logic. It was about remembering.

As she approached, the door opened on its own. No one greeted her. There were no signs or instructions. Mere stillness.

The room had changed again. No tea. No firelight. No chairs. Only a set of stone steps leading downward. They weren't dark or ominous, just unfamiliar. Avery paused at the top, heart steady but alert, then began to descend.

At the bottom, she stepped into what looked like a marketplace, unlike any she'd ever seen. There were no fruits, no fabrics, no spices. No children running between stalls, no voices calling out. There was only stillness. And masks.

Rows and rows of them stretched across shelves and tables. Some were carved from polished wood. Others shimmered like glass. A few looked rusted, as if unearthed from an old battlefield. Some were barely perceptible, like smoke shaped into faces.

Each mask was labelled. Not with a name, but with a role.

- The High Achiever
- The Quiet Child
- The One Who Never Asks
- The Stoic
- The Calm One
- The Indispensable
- The Bulletproof
- The One Who's Fine
- The One Who Can't Fail

People moved through the market slowly, like ghosts. They weren't frantic or hurried. Simply resigned. There was no laughter. No bargaining. No eye contact. Solely motion and masks.

Avery watched as a man picked up *The One Who Always Smiles*. As he pressed it to his face, his lips curved upward. His eyes dimmed, not from sadness, but from surrender. A woman in heels examined *The Indispensable One*, then slipped it on with precision. Her shoulders straightened. Her gaze dulled, just slightly. Another surrender.

A man reached for *The Stoic*. As he put it on, his jaw tightened. His movements stopped. So did his light.

A teenager stood frozen in front of *The Perfect One*, biting his lip. He hesitated, then put it on anyway.

Each mask seemed to fit too easily, as though it had been waiting. And once it settled, the person changed. Not drastically. A slight change. Posture shifted. Breathing shallowed. Energy dimmed.

It wasn't transformation. It was constriction.

Each person looked a little more hollow. A little more like someone trying to be good enough.

Avery's feet stopped in front of a mask that made her stomach twist.

The One Who Has It All Together

She reached out, almost without thinking. It was warm in her hands. Too familiar. Inside the mask, faint words were etched:

You are only valuable when you are holding everything together.

Her throat tightened.

She remembered being ten. Her cousin had been crying during a family argument. The adults were yelling behind closed doors. She'd wiped his tears and whispered, *It's okay. I've got us.* It was the first time she had tried on that mask. And it had fit so well, she'd forgotten it wasn't her real face.

"This one's yours," a voice said gently behind her.

Avery turned.

It was the woman. Same braid. Same steady eyes. Same calm presence that felt more like gravity than guidance. But this time, her presence didn't make Avery bristle. It made her feel seen.

"Do you live here?" Avery asked.

"Not quite," the woman replied. "I travel between thresholds."

Avery hesitated. "Do you have a name?"

The woman's mouth curved. "You can call me Flint."

The word landed like a spark in dry wood. It felt right. A name like earth and fire, not soft or shiny, but real. Reliable.

Avery looked down again at the mask in her hands. "Why do we wear them?" she asked.

Flint met her gaze. "Because they work. They keep us liked. They keep us safe. They keep us chosen."

"Until?"

"Until they start costing more than they protect."

Avery nodded slowly. "And why do we keep them?"

"Because it's hard to let go of what helped you survive, even if it's now keeping you small."

Something clenched in Avery's chest. She hadn't expected the truth to be so quiet. So kind. So devastating.

She looked around. All these roles. All this quiet grief. No one screamed. No one fell apart. They simply put on the masks. And walked a little more like ghosts.

She tightened her grip on the one in her hands. It felt heavier now, as if it remembered everything she had ever tried to carry.

Flint led her to a stall at the very end of the row. This one was different. No shelves. No crowd. Only a single mirror. Above it, a sign read:

No Mask. No Role. Just You.

Avery stepped in front of it.

Her reflection looked back at her. Tired. Unsure. But real.

"What do I do here?" she asked.

"Ask a question," Flint said.

Avery hesitated, then asked softly, "Who am I without the mask?"

The mirror shimmered. Then changed.

She saw herself at twelve, running barefoot through a sprinkler, arms wide, laughing without self-consciousness. Then nineteen, sketching alone in her room at night, music low, no one watching, no one grading. No performance. No pressure. Entire presence.

Then the images faded. And words appeared in their place:

Enough. Even when still.

Avery stepped back, her breath caught in her throat.

"I forgot her," she said.

Flint nodded. "She didn't forget you."

Back at the original stall, a single mask remained. It wasn't polished. It wasn't perfect. It was unfinished, clay, a little cracked. Its label read: *The One Who Is Becoming*

She didn't pick it up. But she smiled at it. And walked on.

That night, back at home, Avery sat at the kitchen table. The image of that last mask: unfinished, imperfect, echoed in her chest. She hadn't touched it. But it had touched something in her.

She opened her journal, drew two lines down the middle of the page, and made two lists:

Masks I've Worn:	*Who I Might Be Without Them:*
– *The Strong One*	– *Unsure*
– *The Capable One*	– *In Process*
– *The One Who Fixes*	– *Real*
– *The One Who's Fine*	– *Free*

She paused. Then added one final line:

I want to matter without the mask.

The compass ticked softly on the table beside her. And turned.

– A path to remembering your wholeness –

The Masks We Forget We're Wearing

Most of the masks we wear aren't chosen.
They're inherited.
Absorbed.
Rewarded.

We don't put them on because we're shallow or fake or weak.

We put them on because they once kept us safe.

There is no shame in that.

Maybe someone needed you to be calm
when everything around you was chaos.
Maybe you became the achiever to prove you were worth keeping.
Maybe you learned early that pleasing others kept the peace, and that peace became your currency for love.

Some masks arrive as armour.
Others arrive as praise.
Either way, they start to feel like skin.

And the longer you wear them, the harder it becomes to tell where performance ends... and you begin.

But here's the thing:

Masks don't only protect. They cost.

They cost presence.
They cost softness.
They cost your ability to hear your own voice through all the pretending.
They cost your peace.

Eventually, you find yourself succeeding... but hollow.
Approved of... but exhausted.
Visible... but unseen.

You're not broken for feeling that way.

You're not behind.

You're tired of carrying a self that
was only ever meant to be temporary.

And that means you're ready.

Not to rip the mask off in some dramatic act of rebellion,
but to start noticing when you reach for it.
And why.

To start asking:

- *Who am I trying to protect?*

– A path to remembering your wholeness –

- *Who taught me this was necessary?*
- *What am I afraid will happen if I let someone see the real me?*
- *Do I even remember who that is?*

The truth?

You're not your mask.

Not even the helpful one.
Not even the one that's made you loved, respected, admired, praised.

You are not the strong one.
You are someone who had to be strong.

You are not the fixer.
You are someone who learned that fixing kept you included.

You are not the one who's fine.
You are someone who thought "fine" was safer than "honest."

But you?
You're more than what you had to be.

And the moment you say:

"I want to matter without the mask," you begin to.

Chapter 6
The Garden of Echoes

Milo's dad picked him up after eight the next morning. They stood in the doorway for a minute, Milo with his hair a little messed, clutching a half-eaten banana in one hand and Frank in the other, mid-story about a lizard he swore was psychic. Avery smiled, kissed his forehead, and watched them walk down the hall.

When the door closed, the apartment felt still. Not empty, waiting.

She wandered back to the kitchen and sat at the table. Her journal was still open. The list from the night before stared back at her.

Unsure. In Process. Tender. Real. Free.

And below it, the line she hadn't been able to shake:

I want to matter without the mask.

She exhaled slowly. And that's when the compass began to spin.

Not fast. Not chaotic. But deliberate, as if it had been waiting for space to move. Then it stopped. Pointing. Not north. Not forward. Simply… calling.

Avery didn't pack a bag. She didn't ask how long it would take. She simply stood, grabbed her jacket, and followed.

The air was different this time. Warmer. Damp. Like early spring. The compass didn't point so much as lean, as if being pulled by something gentle and familiar. Avery followed it down a narrow trail of overgrown vines and moss-covered stones until she reached a tall wooden arch.

Above it, carved in faded script, were the words:

THE GARDEN OF ECHOES

She stepped through.

The garden opened wide and quiet. But it didn't feel peaceful. It felt personal. The air buzzed faintly, not with bees or wind, but with memory. Not sharp, not loud; insistent. She could feel it in her chest, like a song she used to know, or a name on the tip of the tongue.

At first, she thought she was alone. But then she heard it, not voices exactly, but phrases. Disembodied. Soft. Familiar in a way that made her skin prickle.

"You're such a good girl."
"Don't upset them."
"You're so strong, we're lucky to have you."
"Don't be selfish."
"You always keep it together."
"Love means putting others first."

Each phrase landed like a stone in her chest. She didn't remember exactly who said them all, but she remembered how they made her feel.

The garden split into three paths. A wooden sign stood in the centre:

Family – Love – Self

She took the Family path first.

At the end was a clearing with a single wooden bench. Avery froze when she saw who was sitting on it. It was herself, maybe ten years younger. Neat, composed, smiling politely. Eyes too old for her face. Polished like a social media post. Her hands folded in her lap. Efficient. Controlled. Exhausted.

She sat beside her past self and felt a deep sadness rise. Not pity, recognition. The ache was immediate. This was the version of her who carried everything silently. The helper. The fixer. The glue. The one who held it all together while her marriage frayed. The one who smiled at dinner parties and never mentioned the panic attacks. The one who learned that being good was the safest way to be loved.

She remembered driving home in silence, chewing the inside of her cheek raw, exhausted from conversations that felt like auditions for belonging. Back then, she believed love was earned through doing. The more you withstood, the more worthy you were. The more you gave, the more likely you were to stay needed. She had confused being chosen with being useful.

Tears burned behind her eyes. She whispered, "You shouldn't have had to carry so much."

The young woman didn't answer. But her shoulders softened slightly. That was enough.

Avery sat with her for a while longer, not to fix or comfort, but simply to witness. When the air grew still again, she stood, retraced her steps to the fork, and turned to the path marked *Love*.

The garden narrowed. Roses lined the edges, stunning, overgrown, impossible to ignore. Their scent was thick, almost dizzying. It was beautiful. And thorned.

Each step brought back a face.

- The one who told her she was "too much."
- The one who loved her independence, until it made him feel unnecessary.
- The one who said, "I need space," after she finally opened up.

The whispers returned.

"Don't ask for too much."
"You're hard to love."
"You're better on your own."

She reached out and touched a vine. It shimmered slightly, then revealed a memory she hadn't visited in years.

She was twenty-two, lying beside someone who had told her, "I'm not ready for anything serious." She'd smiled and said, "Totally fine," even as her chest screamed, *Don't leave.*

She had learned to be easy to love by needing nothing. That closeness was dangerous. That desire made her inconvenient. She had mistaken invisibility for compatibility.

She looked at the vision of herself, curled beside someone who would never stay. "You didn't need to be easier," she whispered. "You needed to be seen."

The roses shifted slightly in the breeze, as though they'd heard her. The old faces faded, except one, the most recent. The man she had promised forever to. The silence between them had grown so thick that even love couldn't breathe. It wasn't anger that ended them, but exhaustion. Two people mistaking distance for love.

She stood quietly among the roses for a few minutes until a soft peace began to settle where the ache had been. When she finally turned away, the path behind her had changed, opening into the clearing where the last path waited.

The path marked *Self* led to a grove of mirrored pools, round and still, like bowls of silver water nestled in moss. She saw herself reflected in a dozen different forms.

- Laughing barefoot in the kitchen
- Crying alone in her car
- Laughing over pancakes with Milo
- Writing

- Weeping, not quietly, not prettily, only… truthfully
- Watching the world, unseen

Some versions looked worn. Some wild. Some radiant. None of them were wrong.

And suddenly, she understood: these weren't versions. They were pieces. Parts she had hidden, performed, silenced, outsourced. Not because she was broken, but because somewhere along the way, she had learned that being herself came second to being needed.

She stepped closer to the mirror where she stood barefoot, arms open to the sky.

"Thank you for not disappearing," she said. "Even when I stopped looking."

Her reflection smiled. Not in performance, but in peace.

In the centre of the grove was a stone table. On it, a single card:

Love without losing.

She picked it up and held it to her chest. And for the first time, she didn't brace for loss.

As she walked back toward the arch, Flint stood waiting. Her hands were tucked into her sleeves. Her eyes were gentle.

"No thorns in your hair?" she asked.

Avery offered a small, tired smile. "Only on the inside."

Flint walked beside her as they made their way back toward the gate.

"You've spent a long time learning how to keep peace," she said softly.

"Peace outside me," Avery replied. "Not inside."

Flint nodded. "Sometimes we confuse peace with pleasing. Sometimes we confuse love with shrinking. Sometimes we think that not needing anything is how we stay worthy."

Avery stopped walking. Her voice dropped. "That's what I've done, haven't I?"

Flint looked at her. "You learned how to be chosen by disappearing."

Tears rose again. Not sharp. Simply true.

"I don't want to disappear anymore," Avery whispered. "I'm learning to stay with myself… even when I'm with someone else."

Flint reached into her sleeve and handed her another card.

What do you value in relationships – with others, and with yourself?

That night, when Avery returned home, the apartment felt different. Not quieter, it had always been quiet after Milo left, but clearer, like something inside her had been rearranged.

She dropped her keys into the bowl by the door, kicked off her shoes, and stood in the hallway for a moment. Usually, she would dive straight into something: the laundry, the dishes, a scroll through her inbox. Tonight, she didn't.

She moved slowly, almost tenderly, through the space. Made herself a cup of tea she didn't rush. Turned on one soft light in the corner of the living room. Sat on the couch with her legs tucked under her, watching the steam curl from her mug.

She kept thinking about the young woman on the bench. The woman in the mirror. The ache of trying to be enough by becoming invisible.

This journey hadn't cracked her open. It had done something quieter, something deeper. It had helped her remember what she used to know.

Not before the roles or the fear, but before she started believing that love and worth had to be earned. She was not only someone who served, supported, or performed. She was someone who needed, wanted, felt, and longed to be met.

And for the first time in a long time, she didn't want to run from that.

She wanted to meet herself there.

Eventually, she moved to the kitchen table, journal open in front of her, the compass resting beside it. She sat in silence for a long time, then picked up her pen and wrote three headings with values:

I Value

In Love:
Safety. Laughter. Truth. Deep listening. Freedom to evolve.

In Friendship:
Presence. Honesty. No performance. Space to be real.

With Myself:
Compassion. Permission. Stillness. Wholeness. Expression.

She added one final line:

I will no longer love in ways that cost me myself.

And for the first time, she believed she could. The compass pulsed once in her palm. Then turned.

– *A path to remembering your wholeness* –

Love without Losing

Love can be beautiful.
But love – especially for those of us who grew up performing for
connection, can also become confusing.

Because somewhere along the way, many of us learned that love is
*something we **earn**.*

We learn to make ourselves small, agreeable, helpful, "easy to love."
We learn to hide our needs, so we won't be too much.
We learn to merge, to shape-shift, to anticipate.
And we confuse proximity with safety, attention with intimacy,
being chosen with being valued.

In those moments, love isn't love. It's performance.

It's: "If I act the right way, they'll stay."
It's: "If I don't rock the boat, I'll be loved."
It's: "If I take up less space, I'll be easier to keep."

And so, we bend.

We silence our boundaries.
We override our intuition.
We hold space for others while leaving none for ourselves.
We become therapists, cheerleaders, babysitters, emotional shock absorbers, not because we want to, but because we think that's what love requires.

The result?
We stay in relationships that no longer align, hoping things will change.
We lose ourselves trying to hold someone else together.
We call it commitment when it's actually self-abandonment.

But love, real, aligned, conscious love,
doesn't ask you to disappear.

It asks you to **reveal**.

It invites you to stand in your truth,
not collapse around someone else's.

You don't need to be flawless to be worthy
of love.
You don't need to fix yourself before you can be seen.
You don't need to mute your voice, soften your edges, or play smaller than you are.

If a relationship only works when you're quiet, it's not working.

If love requires you to betray your values to keep it, it's not love. It's survival.

So, what does it look like to love without losing yourself?

It looks like:

- Speaking your truth, even when your voice shakes.
- Making decisions from clarity, not co-dependency.
- Asking, "Does this connection reflect my values?"
- Noticing whether the relationship expands or contracts your sense of self.
- Trusting that love built on truth is stronger than love built on performance.

And sometimes, loving without losing yourself means letting go.

Letting go of the fantasy.
Letting go of the version of you who kept holding on.
Letting go of the belief that "staying no matter what" is the highest form of love.

It's not.

Choosing yourself is.

You're allowed to want partnership and freedom.
Support and space.
Intimacy and autonomy.
You're allowed to want a love that holds you,
 without trying to fix, cage,
or complete you.

And you're allowed to rewrite what love
means to you.

Because maybe, once upon a time, you learned love had to be earned.
But now?

Now you know better.

Love that's worth keeping doesn't require self-abandonment.
It doesn't demand that you mask your needs, sacrifice your boundaries,
or perform strength to feel safe.

Love that's rooted in truth is a partnership, not a performance.
It sees you. It supports you. It grows with you.
And it doesn't make room for your wholeness; it wants it.

That kind of love starts with you.

Because when you choose yourself, fully, unapologetically, gently, you show the world how you want to be loved.

Not with conditions.

With clarity.

And when you stop confusing self-sacrifice with connection?

You begin to love without losing.

Chapter 7
The Temple of Time

Continuing to follow the compass, the next place it led her felt nothing like a temple. At first, it was absolute silence. The kind that felt intentional, not empty but waiting. She followed a path carved into pale stone, winding slowly upward until she reached a wide clearing surrounded by tall trees that shimmered slightly in the breeze. In the centre stood a structure, open on all sides and shaped like a sundial.

Above the entrance, carved in stone:

THE TEMPLE OF TIME

Inside, there were no pews. No altar. Only light filtering through slats above, falling in broken patches on the floor like pieces of a shattered clock. Along the far wall stood three stone arches, each framed by worn carvings and lit from within by a different glow.

Above each one was a symbol:

- A clock
- A flame
- A heartbeat

Avery stood still. The air hummed around her, subtle but charged. Each passage seemed to pulse faintly, not in sync, but in rhythm. The compass in her hand stopped moving.

This wasn't about direction. It was about choice.

She stepped toward the arch marked with the clock.

Inside was a long hallway with a moving walkway, like in an airport – only faster. People sped past her, blurry and efficient, gripping phones, water bottles, bags, and to-do lists. She saw herself among them, powerwalking, earbuds in, replying to texts while stirring oatmeal with her free hand.

Go faster. Get more done. Be useful.

A voice in her head, so familiar she didn't realise it wasn't hers, whispered:

If you're not productive, you're not valuable.

She felt it in her chest, tight. That old belief, absorbed early and reinforced often. She remembered being a teenager, curled up on the couch reading a book, when her mom poked her head in and said, "Why don't you help me instead of sitting around?"

Her mom hadn't meant it cruelly, but Avery had learned something in that moment.

Rest meant lazy. Helping meant worthy.

She had spent the next two decades proving she was worth the air she breathed by doing more than anyone asked.

She watched the blur of bodies until even her own image disappeared into the motion. The walkway slowed, then stopped. Silence rushed in. She exhaled, the first full breath she'd taken in what felt like years. When she looked up again, the light had changed, warmer now, flickering. The next arch, marked with a flame, waited.

This next arch led Avery into a dimly lit chamber. Candles flickered low along the floor. In the centre, a woman sat in meditation, silent, still, ageless.

Avery stepped inside and immediately felt awkward. Her hand twitched toward her phone, though she hadn't brought it. She couldn't remember the last time she had sat in stillness without trying to use it, to learn, to improve, to fix.

The stillness here felt unbearable, which, she realised, probably meant it was what she needed.

She sat on a bench and tried to close her eyes. Tried to "relax." But her mind itched.

You should be doing something.
You're wasting time.
You could've answered three emails by now.

The flame beside her flared and dimmed with each intrusive thought. She tried to sit with it anyway. But her breath stayed shallow.

She had been taught to rest only after she'd earned it. To pause only when everything was done. And everything was never done.

On the wall behind the woman was a simple inscription:

Your body is not a machine.
Your energy is not infinite.
Your time is not a transaction.

Avery swallowed. She thought about all the times she had pushed through – exhaustion, headaches, intuition. Times she had worked through illness, smiled through burnout, answered emails in waiting rooms, and written reports with a sleeping child on her shoulder.

Time had always felt like a race. And she was terrified of falling behind.

The flame flickered once more, then steadied, calming her own breath. The candles brightened to a soft gold, as the arch beyond began to pulse, slow, steady, alive. The sound of a heartbeat filled the room, guiding her forward.

She rose, not out of urgency this time, but with ease, and stepped through the final arch marked with a heartbeat.

She emerged into a garden at dusk. The air smelled of rain and jasmine. There was nothing to do. Nowhere to be. Simply the sound of a heartbeat, her own, steady and present.

There were hammocks and soft blankets. A kettle steamed quietly beside a bench. No one was watching. No one was judging.

For the first time in as long as she could remember, Avery sat. Not to journal. Not to think. Just to be.

She wrapped her hands around a warm cup of tea, letting the steam rise against her face. She placed a hand over her chest.

It beat. And beat. Without needing to earn anything.

As the sun dipped below the trees, Flint appeared. She hadn't come through a door. She was right there, as if she had always been.

"Time is not what they told you," she said.

"They told me it was something to manage," Avery replied.

"And?" Flint asked.

Avery looked down at the tea in her hands. "And now I think it's something to listen to."

Flint smiled. "You're remembering."

"I didn't realise how loud time had become," Avery said. "I keep filling it. Measuring it. Trying to catch up to it. But it always wins."

Flint was quiet for a long time. Then she said, "Time doesn't need to be tamed. It needs to be met."

She poured herself a cup from the kettle and turned it slowly in her hands.

"The part of you that's rushing doesn't need a tighter schedule. It needs permission to exist even when you're not producing."

Avery closed her eyes.

Her chest hurt in a familiar way. The ache of someone who had spent her whole life earning rest, and was only now questioning the rules.

Flint reached into the folds of her shawl and handed Avery a soft cloth. Wrapped inside was a small hourglass, but the sand didn't fall down. It floated upward.

Carved on the glass:
Rest is a radical act of self-worth.

When she returned home later, Avery didn't open her laptop. She didn't clear her inbox.

She dropped her keys gently into the bowl by the door, kicked off her shoes, and stood for a moment in the quiet. The space felt softer somehow, as though the day had peeled something rigid off her shoulders. She didn't reach for her phone. She didn't think about what she *should* be doing.

She poured a glass of water. Lit a candle. Sat on the floor.

The cushions gave way beneath her like an exhale. The candlelight flickered gently across the walls, casting slow, dancing shadows.

She didn't need to plan. Or fix. Or figure anything out.

Not yet.

Not right now.

For the first time in a long time, she had no desire to conquer time. She simply wanted to sit with it.

And so she did.

She stayed there for a while, knees pulled in, hands wrapped around the cool glass, heart beating quietly beneath the stillness. Nothing urgent pulled at her. Nothing whispered that she was falling behind.

Later, when the sky had darkened and the apartment settled into evening stillness, she walked to the kitchen table and opened her journal.

She titled the page:

What I Value in Time, Energy, and Health

She wrote slowly:

- *Rest that doesn't come with guilt*
- *Doing less but with more presence*
- *Listening to my body's rhythms*
- *Joy without needing permission*
- *Slowness as a form of devotion*

She paused. Then wrote one final sentence:

I will not rush through a life I'm trying to love.

The compass ticked once in her palm. And stilled, not in confusion, but in peace.

– *A path to remembering your wholeness* –

You are not a Machine

You are not a machine.

You weren't built to be "on" all the time.
To produce endlessly.
To function without rest.
To run at the speed of systems designed without your humanity in mind.

But for most of us, that's exactly what we try to do.

We override our signals.
We ignore our nervous systems.
We caffeinate our way through fatigue and call it resilience.
We pour another glass of wine and tell ourselves we deserve it.
We celebrate people who never stop, and quietly shame ourselves when we do.

We treat our energy like a resource to burn, rather than something sacred to honour.

This isn't a personal issue. It's cultural.
We live in a world that rewards performance and punishes pause.
Where urgency is normalised and rest is seen as laziness.
Where "I'm so busy" is worn like a badge of honour.

But here's the truth:
You cannot live from Cause if your nervous system is constantly in survival mode.

When you're depleted, dysregulated, or disconnected from your body, your choices aren't coming from clarity, they're coming from habit, fear, or collapse.

This doesn't mean you need to quit your job and move to the mountains.
It means you need to stop abandoning your capacity.

Because capacity is the real currency of a conscious life.

And your capacity isn't fixed,
it expands or contracts based on how
well you tend to yourself.

Most people think burnout happens when
we do too much.
But burnout actually comes from doing too much for too long while feeling disconnected from what matters, and from ourselves.

This is why values matter.

When your energy is used in service of something meaningful, something aligned, something that feeds you back, it feels different.

– A path to remembering your wholeness –

You may still be tired.
But you're not drained.

You're not disappearing in the doing.

So, what does it look like to live like a human, not a machine?

It looks like:

Taking breaks before you hit a wall, not after.

Choosing slowness as a form of devotion, not dysfunction.

Creating margins in your day where nothing productive happens, and letting that be enough.

Asking your body, "What do I need? and then actually listening."

It also looks like questioning the systems that taught you worth is tied to output.

You are not your calendar.
You are not your inbox.
You are not your efficiency.

You are a living, breathing, sensing being, and your nervous system was designed for rhythm, not relentlessness.

Let yourself have cycles.

Let yourself ebb.

Let yourself not be "on" all the time.

Because your best work, your truest presence, comes when you are resourced, not depleted.

And being resourced doesn't mean luxury.

It means feeling grounded. Safe.
Spacious enough to respond instead of react.

One of the simplest ways to return to Cause is to pause.
Not forever.

Simply long enough to ask:

- Is this aligned?
- Is this necessary?
- Is this sustainable?
- Am I moving because it's true – or because I'm afraid to stop?

You don't have to earn rest.
You don't have to justify slowness.
And you don't have to perform wellness to be worthy of it.

This isn't about becoming less ambitious.
It's about becoming more conscious, of your energy, your patterns, and your permission to do life differently.

Your nervous system is not a flaw.
It's not a hurdle to overcome.
It's your inner compass.

And when it's asking for stillness, or softness, or breath?

That's not weakness.
That's wisdom.
So start there.

– A path to remembering your wholeness –

Start with one slow breath.
One soft no.
One sacred pause.

And remind yourself:
You are not a machine.
You are something far more magical
than that.

Chapter 8

The Tower of Titles

The sky was grey the next morning. Still and wide. The compass pointed north for the first time. Not with urgency, but with certainty.

Avery followed.

She moved through quiet streets, past shuttered cafes and silent intersections. The city felt paused, as if it had exhaled overnight and forgotten to inhale. A narrow canal wound beside her, leading into a part of town she didn't recognise. The buildings grew taller here, not modern, but ancient. Worn stone, iron-framed windows, and a towering hush that felt like reverence.

At the end of the lane stood a single structure, rising higher than the rest. Its doors were heavy, carved with lines and layers that seemed to fade into each other. It was as if generations of names had once been etched there, only to be slowly erased by time.

Above them, carved in stone:

THE TOWER OF TITLES

Inside, the air was heavy with accomplishment. The walls were lined with plaques and certificates, diplomas and awards. Framed photographs of people in suits, shaking hands, holding trophies, smiling with rehearsed pride.

Each frame bore a title.

- Senior Director
- Founder
- Doctor
- The Youngest Ever
- Most Promising
- Employee of the Decade

Avery walked slowly, her eyes scanning the walls. Some names she recognised. Most she didn't. But what struck her wasn't the titles, it was the expressions. Every person smiled, but only with their mouth. Behind their eyes, the light was dim. Muted. Buried.

A doorway opened ahead, and she stepped through.

This room was different. It was filled with mannequins, each dressed in different outfits: tailored suits, stethoscopes, graduation robes, yoga pants paired with influencer-perfect grins. Each figure wore a sash across its chest, like a pageant contestant:

The Fixer.
The Thought Leader.
The Coach.
The Expert.
The Therapist.
The One Who Helps Everyone Else.

Avery's breath caught in her throat. There she was, not literally, but close enough. One mannequin stood in dark jeans, a tidy blouse, a laptop bag slung across one shoulder.

The sash read:

The One Who Matters Because She Produces.

Her chest tightened.

It was familiar. Too familiar.

She remembered a moment with startling clarity: twenty-four years old, her first *real* job. Her boss had pulled her aside after she'd worked through a weekend to deliver a flawless presentation. "You've got it," he'd said. "This is how you get ahead. Don't slow down now."

She had beamed with pride. Then gone home, ordered takeout, and cried in the bathtub – not because she was sad, but because her body had nothing left to give.

She thought of all the titles she'd worn since.

High Performer. Dependable. Strategic. Safe Hands. Good at Everything.

And somewhere along the way, she'd started to mistake those titles for herself.

In the corner stood a mirror, darker than glass, more like water. Its surface was murky, hard to read. Etched along the top were the words:

Who are you without a title?

She stepped closer. The mirror didn't show her face. Instead, it reflected memories. Not achievements, but moments.

She saw herself:

- Reading to Milo in a blanket fort
- Making art just because
- Sitting on a beach with a friend, listening, no need to fix
- Dancing alone in the kitchen, no camera, no audience

None of it belonged on a résumé. None of it would impress a boardroom. And yet, each memory pulsed with truth. They were full of life. Full of her.

Flint appeared behind her, quiet as ever.

"You've worn your competence like a crown," she said.

Avery didn't move. "It protected me."

"It also limited you," Flint replied. "A crown can become a cage when you forget you're allowed to take it off."

Avery turned to face her. "I don't want to give up what I've built."

"You don't have to," Flint said gently. "But maybe it's time to build something from your truth, not your skill."

She stepped closer.

"Work can be a gift," she continued. "But when it becomes your identity, it starts to own you."

Avery looked at the mannequin again. The bag slung over its shoulder. The calm efficiency in its pose.

"So, who am I without it?"

Flint smiled. It wasn't to reassure, it was to reflect.

"You are more than a role.
You are more than a résumé.
You are the one who shows up. Who feels. Who cares.
That has always mattered more than the title."

Then she handed Avery a rolled scroll. Inside, in delicate lettering:

"What do you value in your work – when no one is applauding?"

That evening, back at home, Avery made herself a peppermint tea and moved slowly through the space. She didn't jump into emails. She didn't outline a plan. She let the stillness linger for a while, long enough to remember the heartbeat behind her ambition.

Eventually, she opened her journal and wrote:

In Work, I Value...

- *Meaningful impact*
- *Integrity over image*
- *Authenticity*
- *Flexibility*
- *Creative freedom*
- *Working in ways that honour my energy, not drain it*

She paused, then added one final line beneath the list: *I am more than what I do – even when I love what I do.*

As she closed the journal, there was a knock at the door.

Milo stood there in mismatched socks and a t-shirt with a glow-in-the-dark dinosaur on it. His curls were wild from the car ride, and there was a smudge of chocolate near his mouth. He grinned like the weekend had already begun.

"Hi, Mom," he said, stepping inside without hesitation.

Avery crouched to hug him, letting the warmth of his little body press into hers. He smelled like wind and peanut butter and something sweet she couldn't quite place.

Something settled in her chest, not only affection, but intention.

This weekend, she wouldn't try to be impressive. She wouldn't fill the hours with productivity or pour from an empty cup. She would show up. Softly. Honestly. As herself.

The compass, resting on the windowsill, turned quietly toward the horizon. And Avery exhaled.

– A path to remembering your wholeness –

Work Without the Amour

Work can be meaningful. Creative. Aligned.

But for many of us, it becomes something else entirely:
A performance.
A place to prove.
A container for our worth.

Somewhere along the way, we were taught that success means being efficient, impressive, consistent, even at the cost of our wellbeing.
So we build careers wearing armour.
We become the high performer. The fixer. The one who always has it together.
We answer emails late, say yes when we mean no, stay quiet in meetings, over-deliver and under-rest.
We think, If I'm competent enough, maybe I'll finally feel safe.

But competence isn't the same as confidence.
And performance isn't the same as presence.

You don't have to burn it all down.
You simply have to get honest.

Ask yourself:

What do I want work to feel like, not just look like?

Am I showing up in alignment... or in armour?

Because if your work doesn't reflect your values, no title, pay cheque, or applause will feel fulfilling.

Maybe you value spaciousness... but your days are packed with meetings.
Maybe you value creativity... but you're stuck in a loop of tasks and templates.
Maybe you value integrity... but you're asked to spin things that don't sit right.

That dissonance adds up.
Not in stress, in
self-abandonment.

Living from Cause in your career means
noticing what energises you...
and what quietly depletes you.
It means redefining success, not as ladder-climbing,
but as alignment-seeking.

It means choosing presence over persona.
And showing up from your depth, not your defence.

So, here's your invitation:

– A path to remembering your wholeness –

Speak with honesty instead of hyper-preparation.

Set boundaries that support your nervous system.

Let yourself be seen, not only as a professional, but as a person.
One with values. Edges. Limits. Depth.

You don't have to be the best.
You don't have to hold it all together.
You have to stop hiding inside your productivity.

That's when your work becomes alive again.

That's when it becomes yours.

Chapter 9

The House of Mirrors

The weekend had passed in the kind of way that stayed with you, not because anything extraordinary happened, but because she had been there for all of it. The pancakes that burned slightly, the rainy walk to the library, the laughter over board games that ended in a fit of giggles on the floor. She hadn't tried to prove or perform. She had only loved. Not perfectly, but honestly.

On Monday morning, she made Milo's lunch while he told her all about a dream that involved skateboards, lava, and a surprisingly wise puppy. He had pulled on his flannel pyjama pants and a hoodie overtop – despite the sun already warming the windows. She let him. Some battles weren't worth the fight.

After the school drop-off, she lingered on the footpath as the last bell rang and Milo disappeared inside. He would go back to his dad's after school, as planned. She had no sessions scheduled. No meetings. No pressure to log in or show up. Her calendar was open, but more than that – she was.

She didn't go home. And she didn't go straight to work.
She walked.

There was no destination in her mind – only trust. Her feet knew the way. She followed the rhythm of her own breath as the edges of the city fell behind her, sidewalks giving way to gravel, then grass, then forest.

The air smelled damp, and the light shifted between trees like something alive.

Eventually, she reached a clearing.

In the centre stood a small stone building. There was no sign, no door, no explanation. Instead, a mirror was set into the wall. At first, it reflected only sky. But as she approached, it began to show her. Not the version with answers. Not the one who had processed and journaled and grown. Just Avery. No edits. No performance.

Above the mirror, in faint lettering, were the words:
THE HOUSE OF MIRRORS

She stepped through.

Inside, the space was circular. The walls were lined entirely with mirrors, floor to ceiling, edge to edge. She was everywhere. Each reflection slightly different.

To the left, she saw herself in her twenties, wild-eyed and overcompensating. Chasing approval with every overachieving breath. The young woman who thought love was a reward and self-worth was measured in gold stars.

To the right, she saw herself in her thirties, a mother, a provider, a machine of efficiency. Tired. Needed. Never quite enough for herself.

Ahead, she met her current reflection. Present-day Avery. Stripped of roles. No mask. No audience. Just breath. Just being.

She walked slowly around the room, studying each version. Some smiled. Some looked away. One wept. One glared. One whispered, "Remember me?"

In the centre of the room stood a single chair. Beside it sat a younger version of herself, the girl under the willow tree, drawing clouds and making up spells.

The girl looked up as Avery approached.

"Did you forget?" she asked gently.

"I didn't mean to," Avery replied. "I was trying to do everything right."

The girl nodded. "You became everyone you were supposed to."

Avery sat.

"I'm tired of supposed to," she said.

The girl reached into her pocket and handed Avery a folded piece of paper. Inside, it read:

You are not your pain.
You are not your performance.
You are not your past.
You are the one who chooses.

The room fell silent. Then the mirrors began to shift.

Each reflection moved, the achiever, the caregiver, the dreamer, the protector, the wanderer. They didn't vanish. They merged. They didn't get erased. They became whole.

Avery stood and looked into the nearest mirror.

She didn't look younger. Or softer. Or wiser.

She looked like someone who had stopped running and started remembering.

Flint appeared beside her, holding a small bundle wrapped in soft fabric. She opened it carefully and placed its contents in Avery's hands: the compass, the hourglass, the stone with *space* still etched into its surface, and a blank map.

Avery looked down at them and spoke quietly.

"I'm not done."

"No," Flint replied. "You're only beginning."

She paused, then added, "Wholeness isn't the end of pain. It's the place where all your pieces are welcome, even the ones you once tried to hide."

Outside, the air shimmered as Avery stepped out of the stone building. The forest was the same, but different. The world hadn't changed. But she had.

Not better. Not fixed.

Whole.

She unfolded the blank map in her hand. And for the first time, she didn't ask where it would lead.

She simply asked, "What matters most now?"

And the compass answered.

Wholeness is the Goal

We spend so much of our lives trying to become someone.
Smarter. Kinder. Calmer. More focused. More spiritual.

We chase healing like it's a finish line, hoping that if we finally fix what's messy, we'll finally be whole.

But wholeness doesn't come from perfecting yourself.
It comes from welcoming yourself.

All of you.
Not only the productive parts.
Not only the polished ones.

The angry parts. The anxious parts. The parts that feel inconvenient or unworthy, the ones you've tried to outgrow or explain away.

You don't have to love every part of yourself right away.
But you do have to stop exiling the ones you've been told don't belong.

That's the work.

Wholeness isn't something you earn.
It's something you remember.

It happens when you stop asking, "What do I need to fix?"
and start asking, "What have I forgotten to include?"

You may see many versions of yourself, the achiever, the people-pleaser, the protector, the dreamer, the child who drew clouds and imagined magic.

Those aren't mistakes.
They're pieces.

The part that over functions? It was trying to stay safe.
The part that lashes out? It was trying to be heard.
The part that numbs? It was protecting you from pain too big to process.

Wholeness doesn't mean those parts disappear.
It means they integrate.

They don't have to run the show,
but they don't have to hide either.

This isn't about glorifying dysfunction.
It's about making room for your humanity.

Because your wholeness isn't in spite of your contradictions.
It's made of them.

You can be soft and powerful.
Boundaried and generous.

Healing and unsure.
Still triggered, and still wise.

The goal isn't to become a perfect version of yourself.
It's to stop fragmenting in the name of self-improvement.

So how do you practice wholeness?
Start by noticing when you split:
- *"I shouldn't still be feeling this."*
- *"That part of me is so embarrassing."*
- *"I thought I'd be past this by now."*

Then soften. And say instead:
- *"This part of me has a message."*
- *"This feeling is here for a reason."*
- *"I can meet myself here without judgment."*

You get to decide who leads now.

You don't owe anyone the version of you they're most comfortable with.
And you don't owe your past self an apology for evolving.

This is what it means to live from Cause:
You're not reacting to shame.
You're responding to truth.
You're choosing from alignment, not old survival scripts.

And you're remembering:
The goal was never perfection.
It was presence.
It was integration.

– A path to remembering your wholeness –

*It was being able to look in the mirror and
say: "I know who I am, even when I'm
still learning."*

*Because wholeness isn't a finish line.
It's a way of coming home.
Over and over.
With more softness every time.*

Chapter 10
The Return

Avery had enjoyed a good few days at work. Not perfect. But aligned. She felt more present in her meetings, less reactive in her inbox, and more honest in her choices. She had spoken up once when she would've stayed quiet previously. She said no to something that drained her. She was starting to trust herself again.

That afternoon, after packing up early, she picked Milo up from school. On the way home, they stopped at the shops to grab ingredients for spaghetti and meatballs, and a big crunchy salad. Milo picked the tomatoes. Avery let him choose the cheese.

Now he was sitting at the counter, legs swinging, tongue sticking out slightly while he concentrated on colouring in a dinosaur scene. Crayons rolled across the bench, mingling with flecks of parmesan and basil leaves.

Avery stirred the sauce, barefoot and relaxed, her journal and compass resting on the windowsill behind her.

Milo looked up from his drawing.

"You look different," he said.

She smiled, setting down the spoon and brushing his hair back from his forehead.

"I think I remembered who I am," she said.

Milo blinked once, then nodded like that was a perfectly reasonable thing to say.

After a pause, he added, "You don't look tired anymore."

Avery's chest softened. "I don't feel tired."

While Milo coloured a masterpiece and the pasta boiled, Avery stood at the kitchen counter with her planner open and a pen in hand. Not to cram more in, but to clear space. She crossed out a meeting scheduled for the next morning. One she'd said yes to out of obligation.

Value: Simplicity. Meaningful impact. Energy that gives, not drains.

That meeting was none of those.

She opened her calendar for the rest of the week. Two strategy sessions. One *networking* lunch. A client she hadn't felt aligned with for months.

She put her pen down. No panic. No guilt. Just clarity.

She had built a life full of things that sounded good, but didn't feel true.

She picked the pen back up and wrote a question in the margin:

Does this honour my values, or my image?

Then she started clearing space.

Later, after Milo had gone to bed, she opened her laptop. Fifty-seven unread emails. Three new meeting requests. One flagged message from her boss marked URGENT.

Her hand hovered over the keyboard.

Then she opened her journal and reread what she'd written days ago in the Tower of Titles:

I am more than what I do – even when I love what I do.

She didn't answer the emails.

Instead, she opened a blank document and typed:

What do I want work to feel like?

Underneath, she wrote:

- *Spacious*
- *Purposeful*
- *Expressive*
- *Free of performance*
- *Aligned with my energy and truth*

Then she opened a new email tab and began drafting a proposal. Not for more responsibility, but for a role redesign. Fewer hours. Different clients. Creative freedom. Integrity over image.

She didn't hit send.

But it was the first time in years that her work felt as though it belonged to her again.

Before she shut the laptop, she opened her email settings and typed an out-of-office message:

> *Thank you for your message. I'm currently in a period of intentional pause and stepping back to reconnect with what matters. I'll respond when I can, slowly, and with care.*

It wasn't for show. It was for her. A line in the sand. A whisper to the world, and to herself:

I'm no longer available for a life that silences me.

– A path to remembering your wholeness –

The next morning, she made a slow breakfast. No emails. No multitasking.

While sipping her tea, she caught herself reaching for her phone out of habit. Then she paused.

Value: Rest without guilt. Slowness as devotion.

She left the phone. Let her mind wander. Let silence stay a little longer.

She took a walk in the sun, simply for the way it warmed her face. No purpose beyond presence.

Later that day, she sent a message to someone she hadn't replied to in weeks,
an old friend from high school who still expected daily texts and long updates.

Not reactive. Not passive-aggressive.
Clear. Kind. Grounded.

Hey, I want to be honest. I've been needing more space lately. Not because I don't care, but because I'm learning to care for myself differently. I know our rhythm is changing, and I hope we can find one that feels good for both of us.

Value: Truth in relationships. Freedom to evolve. Self-respect.

No performance. No apology for wanting clarity.

That evening, her friend Maya called.

"I saw your out-of-office message," she laughed. "You? Taking a step back?"

Avery smiled. "I'm trying something new."

"Like what?"

"Living like my time, and my truth, actually matter."

Maya paused. "You sound… softer."

"I'm not softer," Avery said. "I'm not hardening anymore."

After the call, Avery curled up on the couch with Milo and watched an animated movie she'd seen three times. Not because it was efficient. Because it made him laugh. And because she wanted to.

Value: Joy. Connection. Lightness.

And that night, when she climbed into bed, she didn't scroll. She didn't plan. She simply let the quiet hold her.

For the first time in a long time, she didn't feel as if she was building a life from fragments.

She was choosing. On purpose. From cause.

From *her* cause.

– A path to remembering your wholeness –

Living the Questions

*Most of us were taught to chase answers.
To be certain. Confident. Quick to decide.*

*Certainty, we learned, meant safety.
And doubt? That meant failure.*

*But certainty isn't the same as clarity.
And rushing to answer isn't the same as being aligned.*

*Some of the most powerful moments in a conscious life don't come from answers.
They come from questions.*

*Questions we're not sure how to answer yet.
Questions that don't close a door – but open one.*

Like:

What do I actually want?

What would feel good for me?

Am I choosing this from truth or fear?

If I stopped performing, what would remain?

These aren't problems to solve.
They're invitations.
To pause. To feel. To listen more deeply.

But most of us were never taught how to live with a question.
We were taught to Google it.
Workshop it.
Pick an answer, any answer, just to escape the discomfort of not knowing.

If you want a life that feels true,
you have to stop sprinting toward solutions
that don't serve you.

You have to let your questions breathe.

Because not every question is ready
to be answered.
Some need space.
Some need time.
Some need you to become the version of yourself who can even hear the answer when it comes.

That's not failure.
That's wisdom.

Sometimes, the most aligned response is:
"I don't know yet. But I'm listening."

That's what it means to live the question.

You carry it gently.
You don't force it open.
You stay in relationship with it, not obsessively, but curiously.
You walk with it. You write to it. You let it shape your attention.

And eventually, the answer finds you.

Not because you pushed.
But because you stayed.

You don't have to rewrite your life overnight.
You have to ask better questions —
and pause long enough to hear what your deeper self is trying to say.

That's what living at Cause looks like.
Not control. Not certainty.
But trust.

So, if you're in a season of questions right now, let this be your reminder:

You don't need to force clarity.

You only need to stay in relationship with your questions.

Ask:

What are you trying to show me?

What value are you helping me
reconnect to?

— *The Wizard of Cause* —

*What might I be rushing past in
search of certainty?*

And remember:

**Questions are not gaps in your knowledge.
They're gateways to your truth.**

*The goal isn't to answer everything.
The goal is to listen, with presence, patience, and trust.*

Because sometimes...

The question is the breakthrough.

Chapter 11
The Quiet Yes

Avery had spent the weekend in a rhythm she barely recognised from her former life. A long brunch with friends on Saturday, followed by a walk along the coast. Sunday was slower, a book in bed, a little music, a phone call she didn't rush. No urgency. No over-functioning. Just her, choosing where to place her energy. She could feel her agency returning.

By Monday, the week stretched open again, but it didn't feel heavy. Milo would be home after school. The fridge was stocked. Her calendar had space. There was a steadiness in her that hadn't been there before.

That morning, it arrived – quietly, like most things did now.

In her inbox.

Subject line:
Speaking opportunity – Women in Leadership Summit

She almost deleted it.

It looked like the kind of offer she used to say yes to without question: high profile, well paid, well attended. A panel of industry leaders. A topic she knew well. A hotel ballroom. A well-rehearsed twenty-minute talk on balance and resilience.

She clicked it open anyway.

The email was warm. Personal. They admired her work. They wanted her voice.

And for a moment, the old pull stirred. That familiar whisper: *Say yes. Be seen. Stay relevant.*

But another voice, quieter but truer, rose beneath it: *Only if it's aligned.*

She closed her laptop and made a cup of tea. Sat by the window where the light stretched softly across the table. Then she opened her journal and flipped through the pages where her maps now lived.

- **In Work:** *Integrity over image. Meaningful impact. Creative freedom.*
- **In Time:** *Presence. Rest. Spaciousness.*
- **In Self:** *Truth without performance.*

She picked up her pen and wrote:

If I say yes to this, who am I saying yes as?

The answer came easily.
The old Avery, the one who earned love by over-delivering.

But the idea itself didn't feel wrong. She liked speaking. She loved sharing ideas that helped people feel seen. That part hadn't changed.

What had changed was the way she wanted to show up.

She didn't want to speak from a pedestal anymore.

She wanted to speak from presence. From truth.

So, she replied.

Her message was short and sincere:

Thank you so much for thinking of me. Before I say yes, I'd love to know what kind of space this is intended to be. I've spent the last season unlearning how to perform strength, and learning how to live from authenticity. If that's the kind of conversation you're inviting, I'd be honoured to be part of it.

– A path to remembering your wholeness –

She hit send.

Not with hesitation.

But with peace.

A few hours later, the reply came.

Yes. That's exactly the conversation we want to create. Let's start with a breakout session and see where it leads. Your voice belongs in this space.

Avery smiled.

Not the kind of smile that came from being chosen.

The kind that came from choosing.

That evening, she and Milo baked cookies from a half-crumpled recipe he found in a book. Flour dusted the counter and their noses. Fingers were sticky, laughter constant.

While they waited for the oven timer, Milo looked up from the floor where he was licking batter off a spoon.

"Do people know who you are?"

Avery smiled. "Some do."

He tilted his head. "Like… because you're really smart?"

"Maybe," she said. "Or maybe because I used to be really busy."

Milo thought about that. "Do you still want to be busy?"

She pulled him into a flour-covered hug.

"No," she said. "I want to be here. That's better."

He looked at her for a long moment, then said, "You laugh more now."

Avery closed her eyes and let the moment settle.

Later that night, as the stars blinked through the kitchen window, she opened her journal and wrote:

Today, I said yes – not to opportunity, but to integrity. That's the kind of success I want to grow.

And the compass, resting quietly nearby, turned again.

Not because she was lost.

Because she was leading.

– A path to remembering your wholeness –

The Harder the Choice, The Closer to Truth

The most aligned choices aren't always the easiest.

Sometimes they're the ones that make your stomach clench.
The ones that defy logic or upset other people's expectations.
The ones that don't come with immediate relief, but do come with integrity.

When you start living from Cause, you'll be faced with a new kind of choice:

Do I choose what's familiar – or what's true?

And often, the familiar path looks polished:

- Say yes to keep the peace.
- Say yes to stay visible.
- Say yes to stay relevant.

You'll be offered things that look good on the outside but cost too much on the inside.
Opportunities. Invitations. Recognition. Belonging.

And in those moments, the temptation is real:

- "If I just show up how they expect, this will be easier."
- "I don't want to disappoint them."
- "I've done this before, I can do it again."

But here's the question that will bring you back to yourself:

Do I want to be chosen… or do I want to choose?

Because when you are choosing, from alignment, from awareness, from truth, the choice might not look impressive. It might not make everyone comfortable. It might not even feel like success in the traditional sense.

But it will feel like self-trust.

That's the shift.

You start to value your peace more than approval.
Your alignment more than applause.
Your voice more than your role.

You stop choosing what flatters your image
and start choosing what honours your integrity.

And here's the paradox:
When you lead with truth instead of performance, you often receive

deeper connection.
Not with everyone, but with the people who matter most.

The ones who feel the difference.
The ones who see you, not only the version of you that plays the part well.

You start to magnetise what's meant for who you actually are, not the mask.

And yes, there's risk in that.
Yes, you might lose things along the way:

- Old identities
- External validation
- People who preferred the you who was easier to manage

But what you gain?

- Congruence
- Clarity
- A life that doesn't require constant self-abandonment

So, if you're in a moment where the choice feels hard, good.

It means you're no longer making
decisions from habit.
It means you're being asked to tune into
what's true, not what's expected.

It means your nervous system, your
mind, and your soul are all being
invited to sit at the same table.

This kind of choosing takes courage.

Not dramatic, shout-it-from-the-rooftops courage, but quiet, steady, internal courage.
The kind that says, "I'm going to stay with myself, even here."

So, when the choice feels big, or scary, or uncomfortable... pause.
Ask:

- *What value does this honour?*
- *What version of me is saying yes, the one who needs to prove, or the one who wants to be real?*
- *If no one clapped, would I still choose this?*

And then trust what rises.

Not the loudest voice, the truest one.

Because often, the harder the choice...
the closer it brings you to who you really are.

Chapter 12
The Map Rewritten

Three weeks had passed, and Avery could feel the difference in her bones. Her days weren't perfect, but they felt more honest. She still worked, still parented, still forgot the laundry sometimes. But something had shifted. She said *no* more often, not with apology, but with clarity. She paused when she wanted to rush. She laughed more, even when nothing was funny.

The compass hadn't pulsed since the speaking invitation. But her journal pages kept filling. Her feet felt steadier. There were still moments of doubt, but they didn't own her.

This wasn't a new life.

It was the same life, lived more truly.

That afternoon, with a rare hour of quiet and Milo at his dad's, she sat at the kitchen table with a cup of tea and her journal. The light came through the window at just the right angle, warming the side of her face. She opened the journal and flipped back to the early pages – to the first maps she had drawn.

Each page carried a heading:

- *In Love, I Value…*
- *In Work…*

- *In Time...*
- *In Friendship...*
- *With Myself...*

She read them slowly, almost reverently. Some still rang true. Some felt incomplete. And some had clearly evolved, like seeds that had started to bloom.

She uncapped her pen.

In Love, I Value...
She had written: *Safety. Laughter. Truth. Deep listening. Freedom to grow beside someone – not become them.*
She added:

- *Love that holds, but doesn't grip*
- *Desire that honours the soul, not only the story*
- *The quiet knowing that I can stay... or walk away*

In Work, I Value...
She had written: *Integrity. Meaningful impact. Creative freedom.*
She added:

- *Collaboration, not competition*
- *Work that feeds my nervous system, not solely my résumé*
- *Knowing I'm not here to be impressive. I'm here to be real*

In Time, I Value...
She had written: *Rest. Presence. Spaciousness.*
She added:

- *Margins*
- *The art of doing one thing at a time*
- *Moments I don't have to explain or monetise*

– A path to remembering your wholeness –

With Myself...

She had written: *Compassion. Permission. Stillness. Wholeness. Expression.* She added:

- *Forgiveness for who I had to be to survive*

- *Gratitude for who I am becoming, slowly, imperfectly, intentionally*

- *A daily reminder that softness is not weakness*

Avery leaned back in her chair and looked through the window. The trees across the street swayed slightly in the breeze. A small smile crossed her face. Not because everything was perfect. But because, for the first time in a long time, her life was beginning to look like her.

That evening, she sat on the floor with Milo, surrounded by LEGO pieces. He was building something complex and chaotic, a spaceship-castle-monster, possibly, with total confidence and no apparent plan.

"What are you making?" she asked.

He shrugged. "Not sure yet. I make a little, then do some more until it looks good. You can do it too, Mom. It's fun."

She blinked, caught off guard by the simplicity.

"That's... a pretty good way to live."

He looked up at her, serious for a moment. "Yeah Mom, it is."

She smiled, picked up a few pieces, and began building beside him. No plan, no purpose, just play. For a while, they built in silence, colours and shapes forming whatever they wanted to become.

Later that night, after Milo was asleep, Avery added one more page to her journal. At the top, she wrote:

Living from Cause

And beneath it:

- *I do not owe anyone a version of myself that costs me my peace*
- *I am no longer performing strength. I am embodying alignment*
- *My values are not a checklist. They are a compass. And I'm still learning how to follow them*

She closed the journal and whispered, "This... this is my magic."

The compass on the windowsill turned. Not toward the future. But toward now.

As she reached to close the journal, something shimmered in the corner of her eye.

On the opposite page, one she thought was blank, new words had appeared in the soft, looping script she'd seen before:

You are not here to be perfect.
You are here to be present. To be whole.
To live as the cause, not the consequence.

Avery smiled, not surprised. Just... affirmed.

— A path to remembering your wholeness —

Your Values Are Not a Vibe — They're a Map

Your values aren't aesthetic.
They're not branding.
They're not a vibe you sprinkle over your life like inspirational glitter.

They're your internal map.
They tell you what matters.
They point you toward alignment.
They shape your choices, your relationships, your peace, quietly, consistently, beneath the surface.

Whether you've written them down or not, your values are already running the show.

The question is:
Are you living by them... or against them?

Because when your life doesn't reflect your values, something always feels off.
Maybe not loudly.
Maybe not immediately.

But it shows up as:

Restlessness

Frustration

"I should be grateful, but I'm not"

"It looks good on paper, but it doesn't feel right"

That's the quiet signal that a value is being ignored, compromised, or inherited instead of chosen.

Values can evolve.
Not constantly, but naturally.
They grow as you grow.
Which is why you must return to them,
not once, but often.

Think of them like internal coordinates.
They help you answer:

- *What energises me?*
- *What drains me?*
- *What guides my yes?*
- *What justifies my no?*
- *What makes something feel like mine, even when it's hard?*

When you're living from values, your choices may still be difficult, but they're clear.
You don't need to overexplain.
You sleep better.
You move from congruence, not confusion.

And when you're not?

Even the smallest decisions feel heavier.

So how do you reconnect?

Start with a question:

What is actually important to me here?

Pick an area of your life: work, love, time, health, parenting, money — and ask that question.

Not from your head.
From your body.

Then listen for 1–2 word answers:

Honesty	Flexibility
Freedom	Growth
Safety	Fun
Belonging	Rest
Creativity	Expression

And ask:

Are these being honoured in how I'm living?

If not, that's where misalignment is hiding.
You don't need to burn it down.
But you do need to **adjust toward truth**.

Small steps. Clear boundaries. Aligned action.

Because knowing your values without living them is like carrying a compass and refusing to follow it.

So, make it practical:

- If you value **peace** → stop saying yes to chaos.
- If you value **honesty** → don't stay silent to keep the room calm.
- If you value **growth** → choose the discomfort that invites expansion.

Let your values lead, especially when it's inconvenient.
That's often when they matter most.

They're not only abstract words.
They're reminders of who you are.
And how to come home to that self.

If you ever feel lost, overwhelmed, or unclear,
don't ask what to do next.

Ask:

What do I value here — and am I living like it?

That's the map.
That's your magic.
That's the moment you return to Cause.

Chapter 13
The Cost of Clarity

Living from cause had felt expansive. Freeing, even. But in the weeks that followed, Avery began to notice something else.

It also had a cost.

Not the kind you pay all at once, but in small moments. In pauses that lasted too long. In side glances. In the subtle discomfort that comes when the people around you are used to someone you're no longer willing to be.

She had changed. But the systems around her hadn't.

At work, at home, even with family, clarity created ripples. Not everyone welcomed them.

It started with a meeting.

The kind Avery used to breeze through: sharp blazer, flawless slide deck, quick smile, two steps ahead of every objection. Her role had always been to over-deliver and make it look effortless.

But this time was different.

She had suggested something bold. A shift in direction for an ongoing client project. It aligned with what the client actually needed, not simply what the contract outlined. It was honest. Strategic. Value-driven.

But it wasn't safe.

And it wasn't popular.

"Are you sure that's wise?" her colleague Mark asked, tapping his pen. "They hired us to deliver, not reinvent."

Avery looked around the boardroom table. Some heads nodded. Some stayed still.

Old Avery would've softened the pitch. Diluted the message. Pivoted to make everyone more comfortable. But she remembered what she had written in her journal only days ago:

I am no longer performing strength. I am embodying alignment.

So, she breathed.

And said calmly, "I didn't come here to be agreeable. I came to be real. This direction is more truthful. And more useful."

There was a pause. Not confrontational. Thick with surprise.

Then someone else spoke up. "Actually… I think she's right."

Later, in the break room, Mark pulled her aside.

"Are you okay?" he asked, eyes narrowed slightly. "You seem… different lately."

She smiled. "I am."

That evening, her phone buzzed with a message from her sister.

Hey. Mom said you've been distant lately. Everything okay?

Avery exhaled.

This wasn't resistance like the boardroom. This was softer – but heavier. A different kind of tension. Not professional pushback, but quiet emotional friction. The kind that didn't announce itself, but made you feel as if you'd done something wrong for simply needing space.

She had skipped a family dinner the week before. Not because she didn't care. Not because she wanted to make a statement. But because she had been drained – completely.

Her week had been full of output. And the thought of showing up for another evening of light conversation, subtle judgement, and invisible performance had made her chest tighten. Family dinners were rarely dramatic, but they were rarely nourishing either. A lot of polite updates, unsolicited advice, and tiptoeing around things no one really talked about.

She had chosen not to go. She'd needed quiet. Stillness. The freedom to sit on the couch in pyjamas and hear her own thoughts.

But in her family, absence often read as rejection. The message hadn't come from her sister alone – it carried the weight of the group, the collective murmur of "She's pulling away."

Her thumb hovered over the keyboard. The reflex kicked in fast, familiar as muscle memory.

Sorry! Just busy. Love you. All good. Let's catch up soon.

That message would smooth it over. Keep the peace. Help her slip back into the role she'd always played – the thoughtful one, the agreeable one, the one who didn't ruffle feathers.

But it wouldn't be true.

And she had promised herself: no more false harmony.

Instead, she typed slowly:
I love you. And I'm okay. I've been more intentional about where I put my energy, and sometimes that means stepping back to recharge. I hope you know it's not distance, just care in a different form.

She hit send and set the phone down.

She didn't brace for backlash. She didn't spiral into over-explaining. She let the silence settle, not as punishment, but as clearing. A moment of stillness to mark a new pattern.

Later that night, she opened her journal to a fresh page and wrote at the top:

Living from Cause… when it's not easy

- *I am allowed to disappoint others without betraying myself*
- *Clarity isn't always comfortable. But confusion is worse*
- *I don't need to be understood to be whole*
- *Living my values means walking through weather, not waiting for perfect skies*

As she prepared to close the journal, she noticed something at the bottom of the page. Faint at first, then slowly darkening words that weren't hers, but felt like they came from inside her anyway:

You are not here to be palatable.
You are here to be true.

She exhaled slowly.

It didn't make the discomfort go away. It didn't guarantee approval or ease. But it helped her keep walking. It reminded her that courage wasn't always loud. Sometimes, it was simply not backing down from the truth you've already told yourself.

She looked over the list again. No perfection. No performance. Just practice. Just presence.

The people who misunderstand your clarity aren't always trying to control you. They're used to the version of you who didn't speak this honestly.

Your job now isn't to explain your growth.
It's to keep walking in it.

– A path to remembering your wholeness –

The next day, Milo was getting ready for school when he let out a sharp, frustrated grunt. Avery turned to find him tugging furiously at the zipper on his jacket. It had snagged halfway up, and he couldn't get it loose.

"I hate this jacket," he muttered, eyes already welling. "It's broken."

Avery felt a familiar urge rise to fix it, to dismiss it, to say, *You're overreacting.*

But she caught herself.

She knelt beside him, rested her hand gently on his, and said, "I know it's frustrating. Want to take a breath and try a different way?"

He paused. The heat behind his eyes softened. Then he nodded.

Together, they gently tugged the fabric away from the zipper teeth, found the snag, and pulled it free.

Later that evening, Avery found a sticky note on the fridge in Milo's handwriting. Crooked edges. Red crayon. Slightly smudged.

Try a different way.

She smiled.

And whispered, "Exactly."

You Are Allowed to Change

Let's be clear about something:

You don't have to stay the person other people got used to.

Even if they loved that version of you.
Even if you were good at being that way.
Even if you built your whole life around it.

You're allowed to change.
You're allowed to outgrow patterns, habits, conversations, friendships, environments, goals, and identities that once made sense, but no longer fit.

You're allowed to change your mind.
To soften your stance.
To realise the version of you who said yes back then was doing the best they could... but doesn't need to be in charge anymore.

That doesn't mean you were wrong.
It means you've grown.

And growth is not a betrayal.

It's a return.

A return to truth. To wholeness. To something more aligned than who you had to be to survive, succeed, or stay loved.

But here's what happens when you start to change:

Some people will notice.
And they won't always like it.

They'll say you're different. Distant. Cold.
They'll ask if something's wrong.
They'll try to pull you back into familiar dynamics,
the ones where you over-functioned,
over-apologised, over-gave, and
under-voiced your needs.

And you might feel guilty.

Because you were trained to caretake emotions that weren't yours. You were taught that keeping the peace was your job – even if it cost your authenticity.

But here's the truth:

You're not responsible for staying who someone remembers.

You're responsible for becoming who you actually are.

And that process?

It's not always graceful.

It can be lonely. Messy. Awkward.

You'll second-guess yourself.
You'll grieve versions of you that were good at surviving.
You'll wonder if it'd be easier to go back.

But eventually, clarity will catch up.

You'll hear it in your voice when you speak a boundary without shaking.
You'll feel it in your body when you walk away from something that no longer fits.
You'll sense it in your choices, not impulsive, but intentional.

You'll recognise the shift.
That quiet knowing: I'm not here to rescue anymore. I'm here to reflect.

You won't shrink.
You won't explain.
You'll stand, not on a soapbox, but in your alignment.

That's what change looks like from Cause.
It's not loud.
It's not rebellious.
It's rooted.

And it doesn't need to be explained to
anyone who isn't living in your body.

So, if you're walking through a season
of becoming, if you feel the old parts
of you fading while the new parts
haven't fully formed, take heart.

– A path to remembering your wholeness –

You're not lost.

You're realigning.

Some people won't come with you.
That's okay.

Let them love the version of you they remember.
You're busy becoming the version of you who remembers herself.

This isn't selfish.

This is sacred.

You don't owe anyone your sameness.
You don't owe anyone your sacrifice.
You don't owe anyone the story they prefer over the truth you're finally telling.

You are allowed to change.

And you are allowed to keep choosing yourself, even if it means disappointing the version of you that made other people more comfortable.

Because the point was never to be liked by everyone.

It was to be lived-in by you.

Chapter 14

The North Star

The call came on a rainy Wednesday evening. Avery lit a candle and settled into the quiet, watching the rain trace rivers down the window. The apartment felt warm and still, the kind of stillness she used to fill with noise. Now, she let it stay.

Her phone buzzed: Maya.

She hesitated. The old version of her would've picked up immediately, even if she was drained or halfway out the door. But now, she paused and checked in with herself.

Yes, she had space.

Yes, she wanted to show up. Not out of obligation, but choice.

She answered.

Maya's voice was shaky on the other end. "I don't know what I'm doing anymore, Ave. I'm burnt out. Work doesn't light me up. My partner thinks I'm being dramatic. I'm exhausted all the time. But I don't know what I want instead."

Avery didn't rush to fill the silence. She let it stretch, wide enough to hold the weight of what Maya had said.

Then, gently, she asked, "Can I ask you something strange?"

"Stranger than usual?" Maya offered a weak laugh.

"What do you value – right now – in this season of your life?"

Maya went quiet. Avery could almost hear her blink, frown, tilt her head.

"You mean like… honesty? Health?"

"Not the ones that sound good," Avery said softly. "The ones that feel true. The ones your body says yes to."

There was a long exhale. A kind of surrender.

"I value… ease," Maya said. "Not everything being so hard. I want softness, Avery. I want to stop performing like I'm okay all the time."

Avery nodded, even though Maya couldn't see her.

"Then that's your compass," she said. "If it's not pointing to ease, it's pointing to someone else's map."

There was another pause. This one quieter. Less frantic.

"How did you get so clear?" Maya asked.

Avery smiled. "I got tired of being lost."

After the call, Avery curled up on the couch with a blanket and opened her journal. She didn't feel triumphant or wise. She felt present.

At the top of a fresh page, she wrote:

North Star Moments

Underneath, she made a list:

- *I paused before answering the phone*
- *I asked a real question, not a rescuing one*
- *I reflected her truth back to her, not mine*
- *I trusted that presence was enough*

The next morning, she received a message from Maya:

I cancelled a client today. Just one. But I chose peace over performance. You helped me remember what matters. Thank you.

Avery stared at the message for a long moment. She didn't feel proud. She didn't feel heroic.

She felt aligned.

Not as someone who had it all figured out. But as someone walking her truth, and leaving light behind her, like breadcrumbs.

Later that day, while waiting in line at the grocery store, she overheard someone on the phone behind her.

"I need to keep pushing. Once this project is done, I'll have time to rest."

Avery didn't turn around. She didn't insert herself.

But her whole body whispered:
Or... you could rest now.

She didn't say it aloud. She didn't need to. Not every truth needed to be spoken to ripple.

That evening, she found herself sketching a compass in her journal. The shape came easily. A circle. Four points. Instead of directions, she wrote words that had begun to anchor her:

- *Ease*
- *Wholeness*
- *Truth*
- *Choice*

And beneath the compass, she wrote:

This is how I come home to myself.

As she closed the journal, the compass beside her pulsed softly. Not to guide. To affirm.

A shimmer of ink appeared on the opposite page – the familiar handwriting, soft and certain.

Home is not a place.
It's the moment you choose to belong to yourself again.

Avery touched the page lightly, then let her hand fall to her lap.

She wasn't chasing north anymore.

She was becoming it.

Saying No Without Apology

Saying no is one of the simplest acts of self-honouring, and one of the hardest.

Not because you don't know what you want.
But because someone else might not like it.

We're taught early that no is rejection.
That it's rude, selfish, difficult.
That it causes tension. That it makes us less lovable.

So instead of saying no, we explain.
We soften. We apologise.
We say things like:

- *"I'm so sorry, I've just been swamped..."*

- *"Maybe another time – I wish I could!"*

- "It's not you, it's me."

We try to make our no sound like a maybe.
We try to decline without disappointing.

But here's the truth:

A clear no is kinder than a confused yes.

When you say yes out of guilt or obligation, you don't betray your boundaries, you dilute your presence.

You give from depletion.
You show up resentful or distracted.
You start performing, instead of participating.

And even if the other person doesn't consciously feel it, you do.

You walk away a little more disconnected from yourself.

This is why saying no without apology
isn't harsh, it's honest.

It communicates:

- I trust myself to know my capacity.
- I'm not available for what doesn't align.
- I care about this relationship enough to be real.

You may feel this most clearly in the small moments,
when someone invites you into something that once felt automatic,
and you feel the subtle resistance rise.

You're not punishing anyone.
You're protecting your energy.
You're honouring what you need.

And even if it causes a ripple,
even if someone misunderstands or takes it personally,
that doesn't mean you're wrong.

Because other people's disappointment is not evidence of your misalignment.

It's just their emotional process.

And you are not responsible for managing every emotional ripple your boundary creates.

*You're responsible for **truth**.*

So how do you say no with clarity – not apology?

You get clear on why you're saying no.

- *Is it to protect your time?*
- *To honour your energy?*
- *To maintain integrity with your values?*

Then say no – the clean, clear, kind.

Some examples:

- *"That doesn't work for me."*
- *"I'm not available for that right now."*

- "I need more space than that allows."
- "Thanks for thinking of me, but I'm going to pass."
- Or simply, "no."

No justification.
No scrambling to explain.
No backdoor yes.

And if the other person pushes? You can hold your ground without aggression.

You can say:

- "This isn't about you, it's about what I need."
- "I don't have the capacity to say yes and stay aligned."
- "I know this might feel unfamiliar. It is for me too. But it's important."

Because the more you say no without apology, the more you build self-trust.

You prove to yourself:

- I can choose alignment over approval.
- I can stay in discomfort without collapsing.
- I can honour my boundaries and still be kind.

And slowly, your no becomes less about defence, and more about direction. It stops being a reaction and starts being a compass.

So, the next time you feel that old panic rising, the urge to smooth, soften, explain, pause: Take a breath. And remember: A clear no is a yes.

A yes to your time.
Your peace.
Your priorities.
Your presence.

You're not saying no to be difficult.

You're saying no because you're no longer willing to disappear in the name of being agreeable.

That's not rebellion.
That's alignment.

— *A path to remembering your wholeness* —

CHAPTER 15
WHEN THE OLD SELF CALLS

Avery finished loading the dishwasher when her phone buzzed. The apartment was quiet, the evening soft around the edges. Rain tapped gently on the windows, and Milo was tucked in with a book, humming to himself. She felt grounded. Not euphoric, just steady. As if life was beginning to settle into something more honest.

She dried her hands on a tea towel and glanced at the screen.

A message from her ex.

> *I need to talk.*
> *It's not working.*
> *We need to revisit custody.*

No greeting. No warmth. Only urgency, clipped and heavy, like a door slammed instead of knocked.

She read it again. Then again.

And by the third read, her nervous system had already leapt ahead. Her chest tightened, breath shallow, stomach cold.

He's going to fight for more time.
He's going to say I'm unstable, inconsistent.
Maybe I am. Maybe I've changed too much.

Maybe I'm being selfish.
This is what I get for choosing myself.

The spiral was fast. Familiar. Like a path she thought she'd stopped walking, but somehow found again in the dark.

She stood frozen in the kitchen, gripping the edge of the counter as her thoughts looped tighter.

And beneath all the noise, a younger voice surfaced – old, rehearsed, still alive in the corners of her body.

Just fix it. Make it go away. Be agreeable. Say sorry even if it's not your fault. Keep the peace. Shrink if you have to. Don't let them take something from you.

That voice had been her safety net for years. It had kept her afloat through arguments, tension, loneliness, and quiet threats that had no words but carried weight.

She opened her phone, thumbs moving automatically.

Okay, let's talk whenever works for you. I'm sure we can work it out.

It sounded composed. Cooperative. Accommodating.

It also sounded like abandoning herself.

Again.

She stopped. Closed the message. Walked away from the phone and sat at the dining table where her journal was already open, waiting. Her hands trembled slightly as she flipped to a familiar page:

In Relationships, I Value...

She read the words aloud, letting each one land in her chest.

Truth. Mutual respect. Growth. Boundaries. Space to be who I am.

She whispered the last line again, slower this time.

Then she turned to another section.

In Self...
Compassion. Stillness. Wholeness. Expression.

There was no mention of compliance. No reward for being agreeable at her own expense.

She inhaled. A full, shaky, reclaiming breath.

Her instinct to over-function, to say yes, to smooth it over, to be easy, wasn't weakness. It was the wisdom of a younger version of her, the one who had learned early: if you don't bend, things break. If you speak up, people leave. If you take up space, you'll lose the room.

But she wasn't that girl anymore.

She could thank that survival strategy for what it once made possible, and still choose something different.

So she picked up her phone again.

Deleted the old draft.

And typed, slower this time, from somewhere deeper:

I'm open to talking. But I'd like us to do it with support. This deserves clarity, not urgency. I'm not available to negotiate under pressure.

No apology. No softening. No chasing calm by betraying her own.

She set the phone down and exhaled again. This time, she cried, not out of fear, but relief. She had stayed with herself. That was still new. Still tender. But it held.

Later, Milo climbed onto the couch beside her, curling up without saying a word. He traced the seams of her jeans with one finger, then looked up at her face.

"Mom, are you okay?"

She considered how to answer. "I had a hard moment," she said. "But I stayed with myself this time."

He tilted his head. "Like you didn't run away?"

"Not even a little," she replied.

The next morning, her ex responded.

Fine. I'll ask the mediator to set something up.

It wasn't friendly. It wasn't warm. But it was contained.

And it didn't rattle her.

She had already chosen who she was. No one else got to rewrite that.

That afternoon, she walked by the ocean. The wind was sharp, the kind that pushed into your chest, and the waves slapped the shore with the force of open hands. A younger version of her would have stayed inside, called it too wild, too messy, too much.

But now?

She stood in it. Face tilted toward the grey sky, hair tangled and damp. The elements no longer frightened her. They mirrored her, powerful, chaotic, alive.

"I can do storms," she whispered. "I just don't have to become them."

That night, she returned to her journal and opened to a blank page.

At the top, she wrote:

Who I Am in the Hard Moments?

- *A woman who pauses before reacting*
- *A mother who doesn't parent from fear*
- *A partner to herself first*
- *A listener to her nervous system*
- *A quiet revolution*

She stared at the words, letting them settle. She wasn't proud in a performative way.

She was proud in the quiet, grounded way that comes from telling the truth and standing in it.

And the compass, resting silently nearby, shifted slightly east.

Not to redirect her.

But to remind her – you're still on your way.

Staying with Myself

We often believe that if we're finally living in alignment, choosing better, honouring our values, staying present, life should get easier.

More peace.
Fewer conflicts.
A clear sky kind of season.

But here's what nobody tells you:

The storm doesn't always stop because you're doing the work.

In fact, sometimes the real storm begins after you start showing up differently.

Why?

Because you've changed your response,
but the world around you hasn't caught up yet.

— A path to remembering your wholeness —

You're speaking with more clarity.
But they're still used to your compliance.

You're setting new boundaries.
But others still expect the old flexibility.

You're choosing truth.
But truth can shake things that were built on silence.

That's not a sign that you're doing it wrong.

It's a sign that you're growing.

Storms come when the old ways meet the new you.

It's normal to feel rattled.
To wonder if you're making a mistake.
To second-guess your newfound clarity because
it's not being met with applause.

You might feel it when a familiar
message arrives,
one that tugs at old patterns.
The spiral tries to start.

The scripts return, begging you to bend, comply, make it all okay.

But this time — you pause.
You check in.
You choose from Cause, not from fear.

And even though it's uncomfortable, even though your voice trembles
and your heart pounds,
you stay.

With yourself.

That's what alignment looks like in a storm.

Not feeling fearless.

But not abandoning yourself when fear shows up.

Storms test what you've been building.

And here's the truth most self-help books won't tell you:

You can be deeply aligned – and still triggered.
You can be living from values – and still feel afraid.
You can be walking in truth – and still feel wobbly sometimes.

That doesn't make you a fraud.

It makes you human.

And when you weather the storm without folding into old patterns?
You grow roots.

Not performative strength, but inner steadiness.
Not perfection, but presence.

And the more you ride out those moments without
outsourcing your worth or your choices to external noise,
the more trust you build, with yourself.

So, if you're in the thick of it right now...

If people are misreading your growth
as coldness.

— A path to remembering your wholeness —

If the boundaries are bringing backlash.
If the peace feels distant and the discomfort feels louder than ever...

Take heart.

You're not going backward.

You're learning to stand in the rain without disappearing.

You're building a life that can withstand weather,
not by avoiding it,
but by knowing who you are in the middle of it.

Storms don't mean you're wrong.

They mean you're being recalibrated.

So, breathe.
Root down.
Keep choosing.

And when the wind howls, remind yourself:

"I don't need to control this.
I just need to stay with myself."

That is enough.

That is power.

That is the path of Cause, even in the rain.

Chapter 16

The Invitation

It had been a clear, still morning. Milo was at school, the apartment was quiet, and Avery brewed a second cup of tea.

There was a feeling in the air, not urgency, but momentum. Like something had been shifting beneath the surface and was now ready to emerge.

She opened her laptop, expecting the usual noise – newsletters, notifications, a reminder to update her calendar.

Instead, she saw it.

Subject line: We'd love to have you lead the Keynote.

She clicked it open, her heart already starting to race.

It was from the Women in Leadership Summit, the same group she'd agreed to speak with a few weeks earlier. Originally, they'd invited her to lead a quiet breakout session. A smaller circle. A human space.

But now?

They wanted her front and centre. The opening keynote. The first voice in the room.

She stared at the screen for a long moment.

The flattery was real. So was the risk.

Keynote.

That word had gravity. She knew exactly what came with it.

Expectations.
Spotlight.
Applause.
The subtle pressure to be impressive, articulate, quotable – to perform more than reveal.

A ripple of excitement moved through her. Then a wave of hesitation.

She felt the old split begin to open.

Avery of the past would've leapt into action: scripting, preparing, anticipating. She would've picked the right outfit, written clever lines, and rehearsed a poised vulnerability that made her seem relatable but still polished. She could feel that old muscle twitch.

She even remembered the opener she'd used years ago at a similar event. Tight. Witty. Crowd-pleasing.

Her fingers twitched toward the keyboard.

Then she stopped.

She stood up. Walked to the window. The light outside was soft and cloud-filtered, the kind that made everything feel more internal.

Is this who I am now?

Or who I used to be, trying to prove I was?

She breathed in slowly, pressing her palms into her pockets.

She sat down at the kitchen table, opened her journal and flipped to a page she hadn't filled yet.

What I Value in Visibility.

She stared at the heading for a while, letting the question settle before answering it.

Then, slowly, she wrote:

- *Connection over perfection*
- *Honesty over performance*
- *Saying something real, even if it's not received well*
- *Letting people see me, not only the polished parts*
- *Trusting that I am the message, not just the messenger*

She paused, letting the words sink in.

And then, in the margin, a new line appeared, faint at first, but gaining form as it settled into the page:

Let them see you. The real you is what they came for.

Avery sat quietly with the thought. She already knew her answer. She didn't need to rehearse it or sleep on it.

She opened her laptop, not to begin slides or outline clever talking points, but to respond with the same honesty she had written in her journal.

> *Thank you for the invitation. I'm honoured by the opportunity. I'd love to open the Summit, but only if I can do it in a way that's real. No performance. No persona. I want to talk about what happens when strong women stop trying to be perfect and start living from what matters. If that's the keynote you're looking for — I'm in.*

She read it once more. It felt right.

Then she hit send.

And she didn't wait for applause.

She already knew who she was clapping for.

— A path to remembering your wholeness —

Let It Be New

There's a moment on every journey when you realise:

You're no longer where you were…
but you're not quite sure where you are now.

The old ways don't fit anymore.
But the new ones?
They still feel unfamiliar. Delicate.
Like trying on clothes that fit your soul, but haven't been worn in yet.

This in-between space can feel disorienting.

You're no longer performing, but you're still tempted to.
You're no longer people-pleasing, but the muscle memory runs deep.
You're living more from truth, but you still worry how it'll land.

And in that space, the invitation is simple, but hard:

Let it be new.

Don't rush to define it.
Don't contort it into something familiar.
Don't try to make it look like someone else's version of success.

Let it feel awkward.
Let it feel quiet.
Let it feel unsure.

Because newness is supposed to feel unfamiliar.

When a new opportunity arrives, your old self may want to take over, craft the perfect version, polish every edge, disappear inside the performance. But there's a wiser part of you now. A part that knows: If I do that, I'll be betraying the very thing I've been becoming.

So don't revert.
Don't perform.
Stay with what's real,
and let it be new. That's the choice.

Over and over.

Letting the new voice speak, even when the old one is louder.
Letting your truth lead, even when performance would be easier.
Letting your values shape your yes, even when fear says, "Play it safe."

The world may not always understand.

They'll expect you to show up how you used to.
They'll mirror back old roles, old habits, old labels.
And it'll be tempting to slide back into them, not because you want to, but because they're known.

– A path to remembering your wholeness –

But that version of you?
You did the job.
You got yourself here.

Now it's time to meet yourself again – without the mask.

To lead from the person you're becoming, not the one you've outgrown.

That requires pause.
It requires kindness.
It requires the courage to not have everything figured out yet.

And it requires you to stop demanding clarity from a process that's still unfolding.

So, if your new way of showing up still feels shaky - good.
That means it's real.

Let the words be less rehearsed.
Let the silence stretch longer.
Let the boundaries come out wobbly.

Let it be new.

Because the more you honour it as it is,
the more you build trust in the part of
you that no longer needs to prove.

And eventually, what once felt foreign

becomes natural.
Not because you forced it,
but because you gave it time.

So, the next time you feel that pull to shrink, perform, or default - pause.

Ask:

- *What would it look like to let this be new?*
- *What part of me is growing right now?*
- *What version of me would love this chance to show up?*

Then let yourself.

Not perfectly.
Just honestly.

Because that's what newness asks for.

Not confidence.

But courage.

Chapter 17
The Wizard of Cause

The morning of the keynote, Avery didn't feel powerful. She felt present. She woke before the alarm and let the quiet settle into her bones. She moved through the morning slowly – making breakfast, packing Milo's lunch, brushing a strand of hair from his forehead with intention, not routine. There was no rush, no rehearsing in her mind. Just presence.

She stood in front of her mirror, not to adjust or assess, but to witness. She wore soft fabrics and comfortable shoes. Her hair was half-up, imperfect and easy. She looked like herself.

That was the only goal.

The venue buzzed with nervous energy. Organisers paced with clipboards. Attendees clutched coffee and branded tote bags. Projection screens blinked awake one by one. Backstage, Avery exhaled, letting her heart beat a little faster. It wasn't fear this time, it was readiness.

Flint appeared beside her, silent and solid as ever. No entrance, no explanation. Simply there.

She smiled, a crooked grin full of knowing.

"So," Flint said lightly, "you're the opening act now?"

Avery raised an eyebrow. "Apparently."

"Ready to cast some spells?"

Avery held up her notes, one handwritten page.

"No spells," she said. "Just truth."

Flint nodded. "Same thing, really."

When Avery stepped onto the stage, the lights didn't blind her. She had asked for that. She wanted to see faces. She wanted to remember that she wasn't here to perform. She was here to connect.

She held the microphone like an offering and began, her voice calm and steady.

"Not too long ago, I thought I was successful. I was also exhausted. Disassociated. Disillusioned. And deeply disconnected, not from the world, but from myself."

The room went still. Not tense, rather it was attentive, as though something was leaning in.

"I was excellent at holding things together. I wore being dependable like a badge. I worked through illness, showed up with a smile, and said 'I'm fine' more times than I can count. And I believed that made me strong."

She paused, letting the silence breathe.

"It didn't make me strong. It made me invisible. Even to myself."

A quiet shift moved through the crowd. Shoulders relaxed. Faces softened. It wasn't applause, but it was recognition.

"Then one day, I realised I was living by someone else's map. A map built from expectations, survival, performance, and the fear of being too much. And I got curious: what would my life look like if I followed what actually mattered to me?"

She told them about writing her first list of values, and realising most of them had been borrowed from other people's comfort zones.

She shared how she learned to say no, first with guilt, then with grace. She told them how she stopped parenting from fear, how she stopped overdelivering at work, how she stayed in hard conversations, not to win, but to stay whole.

There was laughter when she shared the story of Milo putting a sticky note on the fridge that read: *Try a different way.*

And then she said:

"Values aren't branding. They're not something you put on a slide or a vision board. They're a compass. And when we follow them, we begin to live from Cause – not from panic, not from performance, but from presence and choice."

There were no dramatic gestures. No pause for effect. Simply her voice, grounded in truth.

She didn't try to impress them.

She invited them home.

After the talk, she stood in the foyer with a paper cup of lukewarm tea and watched small conversations ripple out around her. No one rushed her. No one flooded her. It was quiet. Respectful. Like something sacred had passed through the room and was still settling.

A woman in her fifties approached. She wore a soft scarf and had eyes that didn't need to say much.

"You're like a wizard," she said gently.

Avery blinked. "Sorry?"

"The way you spoke. It was as though you had a compass inside you. As if you didn't need to convince anyone of anything… because you believe yourself now."

Avery didn't respond right away. The words landed, not as flattery, but as something deeper.

The woman smiled again, then added, *"A Wizard of Cause."*

And just like that, the title settled in her chest.

Not as a compliment.

As a mirror.

Later, as she walked through the car park, soft heels on wet concrete, breath steady in her chest, Flint appeared beside her. She didn't speak at first. She matched Avery's pace, quiet and easy.

Then she said, "You've always been a wizard. You just used to cast spells to disappear."

Avery looked over, her eyes misty with truth. "I think I've finally stopped hiding."

Flint nodded. "That's when the magic begins."

They walked together until the car park lights blurred in the drizzle. Then Flint smiled, a knowing smile, and said, "You'll find me wherever you pause long enough to listen."

When Avery glanced sideways again, Flint was gone. But the stillness she'd always carried — that quiet, certain knowing — remained. It was no longer outside her. It was her.

She knew that if she ever needed guidance again, she only had to close her eyes and listen to her heart. The door would appear in her mind's eye, Flint waiting inside, and the compass would point home.

That night, Avery sat at her kitchen table with her journal open and a candle flickering gently beside her. There was no rush to capture it all. Only a steady rhythm to her pen as she wrote on the final blank page.

I used to think power came from performing.
Now I know it comes from presence.

I used to try to change the world by controlling it.
Now I know I change it by choosing – with awareness and alignment.

I am not the effect of my life.
I am the cause.

She signed it simply:

Avery.

W.O.C.

(Wizard of Cause)

Then she smiled, closed the book, and turned off the light.

You Are the Magic

We spend a lot of our lives looking for the magic.

In books. In teachers. In mentors. In moments of clarity.
We chase strategies. Routines. Healing methods.
We wonder: When will it finally click?
When will I feel powerful? Ready? Whole?

But the real magic?
It's not out there.

It's not in a morning ritual, or a perfect plan, or a crystal-clear vision of the future.

It's in the way you come back to yourself.

Over and over again.

Even when it's hard.
Even when it's quiet.
Even when you're not sure it's working.

That's the magic.

Not that you never abandon yourself,
but that you notice when you do... and return.

That's what you'll discover.
Not through a grand achievement.
Not through a perfect pivot.

But through presence.

You stop performing strength and started embodying alignment.

You stop chasing applause and started trusting her voice.

You don't become a Wizard of Cause.
You remember that you already are one.

Because the magic isn't about having
special skills.

It's about:

- *Tuning in when the world says tune out.*
- *Staying soft when you're told to harden.*
- *Choosing your values when everyone else is choosing urgency.*
- *Saying, "This is mine to choose," even when it would be easier to comply.*

The magic is in choosing clarity over comfort.

Compassion over control.

Truth over performance.

And once you realise that... the search ends.

Because you're no longer looking for something to save you.
You're leading yourself home.

And when you do?

Your life starts to reflect it.

Not perfectly. Not all at once.

But moment by moment, alignment begins to show up in your choices:

- *What you say yes to.*
- *What you release.*
- *What you reclaim.*
- *What you no longer need to prove.*

That's real transformation.

Not loud.
Not dramatic.
But undeniable.

Because you'll feel it, in your breath,
your boundaries, your body.

You'll wake up one day and realise:
I like who I am when I'm not performing.

You'll look back and see a trail of moments where you stayed.
With your heart.

— A path to remembering your wholeness —

With your values.
With your truth.

And that's when you know:

You didn't just learn a new mindset.
You became someone new,
by remembering what was always there.

So, if you've been waiting for someone to hand you the wand, the plan, the formula...

This is it.

This is the moment.

Not because everything is figured out.

But because you are finally in the room with yourself.

That is the spell.
That is the turning point.
That is the real, quiet revolution.

You don't need a title. Or a badge. Or an audience.

You need to keep choosing.

From presence. From alignment. From cause.

And you'll realise:

You were the magic all along.

Chapter 18
The Map Continues

It was a slow Sunday morning. Rain moved down the windows in soft ribbons. The scent of bacon drifted through the apartment.

Milo sat on the couch, legs tucked underneath him, deeply focused on a video game. His tongue poked slightly from the corner of his mouth, eyes tracking the screen with the kind of full-bodied attention that only eight-year-olds can summon.

Avery sat cross-legged on the floor with a cup of coffee in her hands and her journal open in her lap. She wasn't writing. She was rereading.

The pages were worn now, corners bent, ink smudged where her fingers had lingered. What began as scribbled attempts to figure herself out had become something sacred. A trail map. Drawn by instinct. Annotated with truth. A quiet record of who she was when she finally stopped performing.

Across the room, Milo looked up from his game. "Can I have a journal too?"

Avery blinked, caught off guard. "What for?"

He shrugged. "You always look calm when you write in it. I want to write stuff too. Like things I like. And things I don't."

She smiled, heart swelling. "That's exactly how maps get made."

She stood and walked to her room. On the shelf was a stack of blank notebooks she had once collected in the hope that more pages might make her feel more complete. She picked one with a simple blue cover and brought it back to him.

Milo paused his game and took the notebook in both hands as though it was a treasure. He turned to the first page, grabbed a pencil, and mustered his concentration. Then, slowly, he wrote:

My Favourite Things

Then, in his slanted, careful handwriting:

- *Pancakes*
- *Mom*
- *Dad*
- *Spinning in circles*
- *Drawing dragons*
- *Being by myself*
- *People who don't lie*

Avery blinked back tears. Not from pride. From recognition. He was already living at Cause. He just didn't have the language for it yet.

That afternoon, she met Maya for tea at the park. They sat on a bench beneath the grey, open sky, sipping from paper cups while clouds rearranged themselves overhead. Their conversation was light at first, the kind that settles the nervous system. Then Maya turned, her voice soft.

"I told my boss I'm taking a month off. No plan. I need space."

Avery raised her eyebrows. "Look at you."

Maya exhaled. "I don't know what I'm doing. But for the first time, I think that's the point."

Avery nodded slowly. "You're not lost. You're just off the old map."

Maya smiled and reached into her bag. She pulled out a small black notebook and handed it to Avery. "I started writing down what I value. You started a trend."

After walking Maya back to her car with a long hug and no need for extra words, Avery returned home and moved quietly through the apartment. The space felt calm, lived-in, and hers.

She walked to the bookshelf where her first journal now lived. Reaching up, she picked up the compass Flint had given her and held it for a moment. The metal was warm in her hand, familiar.

She placed it beside the journal, no longer needing it in her pocket. Its direction had become internal.

She took a small blank card and wrote in clear lettering:

The compass only responds when you do.

Then she tucked the card into the back of Milo's new journal. Not for now. For someday.

That night, after bedtime stories and three questions about stars, Milo drifted to sleep. Avery stood by his door for a moment, listening to the rhythm of his breath. The air felt full. Alive. Honest.

She walked to the window and looked out over the city, its lights flickering like a field of distant fireflies. She placed a hand gently on the glass and whispered, not to herself exactly, and not to the night, but to something deeper.

"The map continues."

Behind her, resting quietly on the windowsill, the compass shifted one final time.

— A path to remembering your wholeness —

Not forward.

Not backward.

Just inward.

You Are Not Behind

If you're holding this book, you've already started.

You may not feel ready.
You may not feel clear.
You may still be figuring out where you end, and the world begins.

That's okay.

Clarity isn't a lightning bolt. **It's a practice.**
Cause isn't a destination. **It's a return.**
To your breath.
To your voice.
To your feet on the ground.

You are not behind.
You are becoming.

Not perfect. Not polished.
But honest.
Present.
Free.

The world doesn't reward becoming.
It rewards consistency, performance, certainty.
But you're not here to repeat yourself.
You're here to remember yourself.

And that remembering?

It won't always look dramatic.
It won't always be Instagrammable.
It might look like cancelling a call.
Saying no without guilt.
Choosing rest when your mind says hustle.
Taking a walk without your phone.
Pausing before replying.
Asking, **"What do I actually want?"**

This life, your one, unrepeatable, extraordinary life,
will not wait for you to feel fully prepared.
It will respond the moment you respond to yourself.

So, take one step.
Then another.
Then another.

— The Wizard of Cause – A path to remembering your wholeness —

Let your values be the compass.
Let your truth be the map.
Let your presence be the magic.

You don't need a title.
You don't need permission.
You don't need a crown.

You already hold the power.

You are the Wizard of Cause.

And this?

This is just the beginning.

— *A path to remembering your wholeness* —

REFLECTIONS AND PROMPTS

You've walked with Avery.

You've witnessed her unmask, unlearn, and return to herself – one value, one breath, one honest moment at a time.

Now it's your turn.

This section is not a checklist. It's not a test. It's a mirror.

Each prompt is an invitation – not to fix yourself, but to notice:

Where have I been living from Effect?

Where do I want to return to Cause?

What really matters to me… in this season?

You don't have to answer everything now. You don't have to rush clarity.

Let this part be quiet.
Let it be yours.
Let it guide you home.

As you move through these reflections, remember, you don't have to do this alone. Transformation isn't about perfection; it's about practice, support, and staying connected to what matters.

If you'd like a little more guidance, visit **wizardofcause.com** where you'll find videos and resources to help you deepen this work and learn how to live from Cause in your everyday life.

And if you're ready to go further, you can work directly with **me** or one of **my Wizards** - coaches specially trained in the principles of *The Wizard of Cause*. They'll help you uncover your values, realign your map, and live in alignment with your own truth: one choice, one breath, one brave step at a time.

Because sometimes, all it takes is a conversation to remind you that you already have the compass, and we just help you learn how to follow it.

SELF

I am not something to be improved. I am someone to come home to.

Reflect:

- When do I feel most like *myself?*
- What masks have I worn to be accepted?
- Who was I before I learned I needed to earn love or belonging?
- What parts of me am I ready to reclaim?

Map It:

What masks have you worn that no longer serve you?

What titles do you have? What would be useful to release?

Where are you living in <u>effect</u> in the area of SELF?

In my relationship with myself, I value...
(List 3–5 values that feel true for you, not ideal, but real.)

Value (What is important to you?)	Is it met? Y/N?

For the values being met, what can you continue doing, being, or having to get these values met?

For the values <u>not</u> being met, what can you start doing, being, or having to get these values met?

For the values <u>not</u> being met, what can you change doing, being, or having to get these values met?

When you are living at <u>cause</u> in the area of SELF what will you notice, what will be different or enhanced?

TIME & ENERGY

I will not rush through a life I'm trying to love.

Reflect:

- What drains me that I continue to tolerate?
- What rhythms feel most natural to me?
- Where in my life am I moving too fast, and why?
- What would change if I believed I didn't have to earn rest?

Map It:

What is happening with your time and energy that is no longer serving you?

Where do you spend the majority of your time and energy?

Where are you living in <u>effect</u> in the area of TIME & ENERGY?

When it comes to my time and energy, I value...

(List 3–5 values that feel true for you, not ideal, but real.)

Value (What is important to you?)	Is it met? Y/N?

For the values being met, what can you continue doing, being, or having to get these values met?

For the values not being met, what can you start doing, being, or having to get these values met?

For the values not being met, what can you change doing, being, or having to get these values met?

When you are living at cause in the area of **TIME & ENERGY** what will you notice, what will be different or enhanced?

WORK

I used to think success meant being everything. Now I know it means being aligned.

Reflect:

- Where in my work life am I performing instead of expressing?
- What roles or titles have I tied my worth to?
- What do I want work to *feel* like – not only what I want to do?
- What would I still choose to do, even if no one applauded?

Map It:

What masks have you worn that no longer serve you?

What titles do you have? What would be useful to release?

Where are you living in <u>effect</u> in the area of WORK?

When it comes to my work, I value…
(List 3–5 values that feel true for you, not ideal, but real.)

Value (What is important to you?)	Is it met? Y/N?

For the values being met, what can you continue doing, being, or having to get these values met?

For the values <u>not</u> being met, what can you start doing, being, or having to get these values met?

For the values <u>not</u> being met, what can you change doing, being, or having to get these values met?

When you are living at <u>cause</u> in the area of WORK what will you notice, what will be different or enhanced?

RELATIONSHIPS

I will no longer love in ways that cost me myself.

Reflect:

- What did I learn love was *supposed* to look like?
- What voices shaped my beliefs about being needed, liked, or wanted?
- Where do I abandon my truth to maintain connection?
- What does safe, nourishing connection feel like to *me*?

Map It:

What masks have you worn that no longer serve you in relationships?

What beliefs do you hold that may need to be released?

Where are you living in <u>effect</u> in the area of RELATIONSHIPS?

In my relationships, I value…
(You may wish to list different values for romantic, family, friendship, etc.)

Value (What is important to you?)	Is it met? Y/N?

For the values being met, what can you continue doing, being, or having to get these values met?

For the values <u>not</u> being met, what can you start doing, being, or having to get these values met?

For the values <u>not</u> being met, what can you change doing, being, or having to get these values met?

When you are living at <u>cause</u> in the area of RELATIONSHIPS what will you notice, what will be different or enhanced?

PARENTING & LEGACY

Children don't follow what we say. They inherit how we live.

(Whether you're a parent, mentor, guide, or leader – this is about what you pass on through how you live.)

Reflect:

- What do I model with my behaviour, not only my words?
- What do I want the people I care for to learn from how I live?
- What survival strategies did I inherit that I no longer wish to pass down?
- What do I hope becomes *contagious* about the way I move through the world?

Map It:

What behaviours or habits are you modelling for others that are not useful?

What stories from your past are you still living that may be holding you back?

Where are you living in <u>effect</u> in the area of PARENTING & LEGACY?

As a parent, I value…
(You may also want to look at this as a mentor, guide, leader, etc.)

Value (What is important to you?)	Is it met? Y/N?

For the values being met, what can you continue doing, being, or having to get these values met?

For the values <u>not</u> being met, what can you start doing, being, or having to get these values met?

For the values <u>not</u> being met, what can you change doing, being, or having to get these values met?

When you are living at <u>cause</u> in the area of PARENTING & LEGACY what will you notice, what will be different or enhanced?

VISIBILITY & EXPRESSION

I'm not here to impress. I'm here to express.

Reflect:

- Where do I shrink, edit, or polish myself to feel accepted?
- What part of me longs to be seen – not celebrated, simply *witnessed*?
- How do I express myself when I'm not trying to be impressive?
- What would it mean to take up space without apology?

Map It:

What parts of you do you hide from others or not express freely?

What masks have you worn that no longer serve you in being visible?

What beliefs do you hold that may need to be released?

Where are you living in <u>effect</u> in the area of VISIBILITY & EXPRESSION?

When I let myself be seen, I value…
(List 3–5 values that feel true for you, not ideal, but real.)

Value (What is important to you?)	Is it met? Y/N?

For the values being met, what can you continue doing, being, or having to get these values met?

For the values <u>not</u> being met, what can you start doing, being, or having to get these values met?

For the values <u>not</u> being met, what can you change doing, being, or having to get these values met?

When you are living at <u>cause</u> in the area of **VISIBILITY & EXPRESSION**, what will you notice, what will be different or enhanced?

EMOTIONAL HEALTH

You are not a machine. Your nervous system is not a flaw, it's your compass.

Reflect:

- What signals does my body give me when something is out of alignment?
- When do I override my own needs – and why?
- What does it feel like to be regulated, grounded, or resourced?
- What kind of rest, movement, or slowness supports my nervous system?

Map It:

What life situations put you out of alignment with your emotional health?

What beliefs do you hold about emotional health that may need to be released?

Where are you living in <u>effect</u> in the area of EMOTIONAL HEALTH?

When it comes to emotional health, I value…
(List 3–5 values that feel true for you, not ideal, but real.)

Value (What is important to you?)	Is it met? Y/N?

For the values being met, what can you continue doing, being, or having to get these values met?

For the values <u>not</u> being met, what can you start doing, being, or having to get these values met?

For the values <u>not</u> being met, what can you change doing, being, or having to get these values met?

When you are living at <u>cause</u> in the area of EMOTIONAL HEALTH, what will you notice, what will be different or enhanced?

PHYSICAL HEALTH

Your body is not a project to perfect. It's a home to inhabit.

Reflect:

- When do I feel most alive, strong, or connected in my body?
- Where do I treat my body like a problem to fix instead of a partner to listen to?
- How do my choices around food, movement, and rest reflect my values?
- What messages from my body have I been overriding, postponing, or numbing?
- What might change if I approached health as collaboration, not control?

Map It:

What choices do you make about your health that are not sustaining you?

What beliefs about health do you hold that may need to be released?

Where are you living in <u>effect</u> in the area of PHYSICAL HEALTH?

When it comes to physical health, I value…

(List 3–5 values that feel true for you, not ideal, but real.)

Value (What is important to you?)	Is it met? Y/N?

For the values being met, what can you continue doing, being, or having to get these values met?

For the values <u>not</u> being met, what can you start doing, being, or having to get these values met?

For the values <u>not</u> being met, what can you change doing, being, or having to get these values met?

When you are living at <u>cause</u> in the area of **PHYSICAL HEALTH**, what will you notice, what will be different or enhanced?

FINANCE & MONEY

Money is not your worth. It's a mirror for how you give, receive, and trust.

Reflect:

- What stories did I inherit about money from family, culture, or past experience?
- When do I feel empowered with money, and when do I feel fearful or avoidant?
- How do I use money to express my values, or to seek safety or approval?
- Where am I spending out of habit, guilt, or comparison instead of alignment?
- What would change if I treated money as energy, something to circulate with intention rather than control with fear?

Map It:

What behaviours or habits are you modelling for others that are not useful?

What stories from your past are you still living that may be holding you back?

Where are you living in <u>effect</u> in the area of FINANCE & MONEY?

In my relationship with finance and money, I value…
(List 3–5 values that feel true for you, not ideal, but real.)

Value (What is important to you?)	Is it met? Y/N?

For the values being met, what can you continue doing, being, or having to get these values met?

For the values <u>not</u> being met, what can you start doing, being, or having to get these values met?

For the values <u>not</u> being met, what can you change doing, being, or having to get these values met?

When you are living at <u>cause</u> in the area of FINANCE & MONEY, what will you notice, what will be different or enhanced?

BOUNDARIES & CHOICE

The moment you stop saying 'I have to...' and start asking 'Do I want to?' you move toward your power.

Reflect:

- Where am I making choices out of obligation, not alignment?
- What boundaries am I afraid to set, and what am I protecting by not setting them?
- When have I said yes to avoid disappointing someone else?
- What value am I protecting when I say no?

Map It:

Where and when do you not protect your boundaries?

What beliefs do you have about enforcing your boundaries?

Where are you living in <u>effect</u> in the area of BOUNDARIES & CHOICES?

When it comes to boundaries and choices, I value…
(List 3–5 values that feel true for you, not ideal, but real.)

Value (What is important to you?)	Is it met? Y/N?

For the values being met, what can you continue doing, being, or having to get these values met?

For the values <u>not</u> being met, what can you start doing, being, or having to get these values met?

For the values <u>not</u> being met, what can you change doing, being, or having to get these values met?

When you are living at <u>cause</u> in the area of BOUNDARIES, what will you notice, what will be different or enhanced?

— A path to remembering your wholeness —

MY CAUSE, MY COMPASS

Values aren't rules. They're reminders. Portals. Anchors. Invitations.

This is not the end of your story. This is the map you carry forward.

The compass only responds when *you do.*

It won't always feel easy. But it will always feel **like you.**

My Compass:

From <u>all</u> of the values you have written on the previous pages, write down the values that repeat 2 or more times. These are often your core values that feel most alive, true, and trustworthy — the ones that will guide your next season.

-
-
-
-
-

And then, in your own words:

I choose to live from Cause by…

And I will remind myself of this by…
(Name a ritual, phrase, prompt, anchor, or practice you can return to.)

NOTES

– A path to remembering your wholeness –

NOTES

MEET THE AUTHOR
DR. HEIDI HERON PSYD

Dr. Heidi Heron is a psychologist, Master NLP Trainer, and spiritual teacher whose work sits at the intersection of psychology, consciousness, and human potential. Since the late 1990s, she has been helping people uncover the deeper patterns that shape their lives, not just to change their thinking but to return home to themselves.

American by birth and now based in Sydney, Australia, Heidi is internationally recognised for her leadership in the field of Neuro-Linguistic Programming (NLP). As the co-founder of NLP Worldwide, she has trained thousands of coaches, therapists, and leaders across the globe, helping them to use NLP as a pathway for healing, growth, and authentic living. She is an advocate for professional standards and ethics in practice, contributing her time to several leadership boards. Her background includes a Doctorate in Clinical Psychology, a Master's in Adult Education, and a Master's in Consciousness, giving her a uniquely integrative approach to transformation—one that honours both the science of mind and the mystery of spirit.

While her professional career has been rich with teaching, therapy, coaching, and mentoring, *The Wizard of Cause* marks a deeply personal evolution in her work. The book grew from decades of witnessing what happens when people live by someone else's map, chasing achievement, approval, or belonging, only to realise they have lost touch with their own compass. As both a therapist and a human being, Heidi has observed that our lives become most aligned when we return to the values that truly matter to us.

At the heart of her philosophy is a simple yet powerful idea: we thrive when we get most of our values met most of the time. Values, she teaches, are not lofty ideals to aspire to someday; they are the essential ingredients that give life meaning right now. When we know what we stand for and live in alignment with it, life stops feeling like a performance and starts feeling like home.

The Wizard of Cause was born from that truth. It began as a reflection on the countless clients and students who had all the outer markers of success but still felt unfulfilled, as well as on her own moments of realising that doing "everything right" does not always feel right. She reminds us that awakening is not about becoming someone new; it is about remembering who we have always been. That remembrance, she believes, begins with self-awareness and deep compassion. "The moment you stop living in reaction to life and start creating from authenticity," she says, "is the moment you come back to Cause, where freedom, choice, and wholeness live."

Throughout her career, Heidi has balanced her professional mastery with a deep love of learning and human connection. She describes herself as both a scientist and a seeker, equally at home in conversations about neuroscience as in discussions about spirituality and purpose. This dual lens infuses her work with grounded wisdom. Her therapy, coaching, and teaching are marked by a rare blend of insight, humour, and presence—qualities that make her approachable even when exploring profound truths.

Beyond her professional life, Heidi is an avid traveller, golfer, and lifelong student of consciousness. She has lived and worked across continents, from Australia to the Middle East to the United States, learning from cultures and traditions that view the mind and spirit as inseparable. Her approach to growth is not about perfection but about presence—about learning to live intentionally, compassionately, and in alignment with one's true self.

As Heidi often says to her students, "People don't change; they become more of who they truly are." *The Wizard of Cause* is an invitation to do exactly that.

To explore your own journey of alignment and self-discovery, you can work 1:1 with Dr. Heidi or one of her Wizard Coaches. Visit **wizardofcause.com** to learn more and take the next step in becoming your own Wizard of Cause.

www.ingramcontent.com/pod-product-compliance
Lightning Source LLC
Chambersburg PA
CBHW061728070526
44583CB00024B/3048